A FIELD GUIDE TO THE
WILDLIFE
of
NORTH AMERICA

A FIELD GUIDE TO THE
WILDLIFE
of
NORTH AMERICA

Bryan Richard

Bath • New York • Singapore • Hong Kong • Cologne • Delhi • Melbourne

This edition published in 2009

Parragon
Queen Street House
4 Queen Street
Bath, BA1 1HE, UK

Produced by Atlantic Publishing

Photographs courtesy of
Photolibrary.com
(see page 256 for copyright details)
Text © Parragon Books Ltd 2006

ISBN 978-1-4075-7449-3

Printed in China

CONTENTS

INTRODUCTION

From the snowy tundra of Alaska, down to the wetlands of Florida and right through the rather more arid Great Plains, the diverse habitats of North America from coast to coast teem with life at every possible level of the environmental web. The many entries in this Field Guide have been chosen to celebrate this diversity and provide a rich cross-section of North American wildlife, from the largest mammals to the smallest insects. Included here are many of the most common and the most remarkable of the multiplicity of fauna that inhabit the land, waters and skies of North America: from the Bald Eagle, that soaring, majestic bird symbolic of US national identity, to the Honey Bee, and the Carpenter Ant. The Bison, another animal almost synonymous with North America, is here – and so is the House Fly, common throughout the world.

Identification
Identifying an individual species can give you a sense of achievement, and this Field Guide aims to encourage readers to look at the wildlife around them and find out more. The species selected for inclusion are illustrated in photographs with a stunning clarity that aids identification of even the smallest animal. The beauty of a Painted Lady butterfly is captured as vividly as the majesty and splendor of the Polar Bear or the dangerous elegance of the Eastern Coral Snake. The striking colors of birds like the Northern Cardinal, the Scarlet Tanager and the Indigo Bunting are clearly shown, but the more subtle plumage of the Song Sparrow is equally well illustrated.

In addition to the visual images for each creature, information panels specify the size, have a brief description, describe the habitat, and give ways to distinguish between similar species. These details are further elaborated through longer explanations about lifestyles, life cycles, social organization and behavior. We come to understand that the Star-nosed Mole is highly aquatic, eating small fish as well as earthworms and insects, but is also able to live off fat reserves in its tail when frozen ground makes burrowing for food difficult. Or take the flamboyant and noisy Blue Jay; not only does it have a harsh voice, it also imitates the calls of other birds, and is particularly good at copying the Red-shouldered Hawk. The Sea Otter's tool-using skills are described, as is the impressive spring display of the Sage Grouse… and there's more.

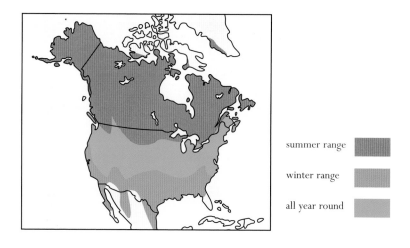

summer range

winter range

all year round

Range maps

A series of maps which are inset into the photographs indicates habitat and range for those mammals, reptiles, birds, insects and fish not found across the whole of North America. For migratory creatures such as the Canada Goose or the Common Loon, maps are color-coded to show winter, summer and all-year-round ranges: green for all-year-round; red for summer; blue for winter. Although some animals do make slight variations in range when the vagaries of weather or their own innate positioning systems take them off course, the maps will show the most likely species within a particular area. As such they can be useful means of making decisive identification; to take an extreme example, though the Kit Fox and the Arctic Fox are superficially similar at some times of year, their ranges are very different. Some species don't have range maps; this happens rarely and is the case where there is not sufficient information to draw up accurate ones in which readers can have complete confidence.

Scope and Groupings

Although in any comparatively concise Field Guide it is not possible to incorporate every single species of creature to be found in North America, a wide scope and array is included here which provides an insight into the extraordinarily varied wildlife of these lands. There are sections on mammals, reptiles, amphibians, fish, invertebrates and birds. For details on the latter category much gratitude is due to Michael Vanner, author of *The Encyclopedia of North American Birds.*

Within each of these sections individual species are, wherever possible, grouped according to their taxonomic relationships. The main heading for each entry gives the common name together with the scientific, or Latin, name. The scientific name is given in two parts: the first part, the genus, which indicates a closely related group, and the second part, the species name which identifies a specific creature. Thus in *Ursus arctos*, *Ursus* describes a bear and *arctos* indicates specifically the Grizzly or Brown Bear, as opposed to *Ursus americanus*, the Black Bear, and *Ursus maritimus*, the Polar Bear. Or take the wolves: *Canis lupus* is the Gray Wolf and *Canis rufus* the Red Wolf. Sometimes an animal or bird will have a third part to its scientific name, identifying a sub-species, but this level of difference cannot usually be easily observed in the wild. The major advantage of Latin names is that they are universal, describing the same animal in any language.

Ethics and Conservation

Anyone out watching wildlife must be aware of their own behavior. Observing wild animals in their environment is a fascinating and rewarding experience but it is important to consider that any human presence will have an impact upon a creature's life, behavior and habitat. Although it is impossible to avoid some disturbance, try to minimize it and be aware that actions such as making excessive noise, leaving litter, trampling brush or grass can have seriously detrimental effects. Remember too that while observing one species you could be causing damage to the habitat of another in nature's delicate web, so be circumspect and careful. Never do anything that might compromise a habitat. Some species have only disappeared because their habitat was damaged or destroyed by human intervention and over the last few hundred years many North American species have become extinct as a result of human activity. Many more have become endangered; Loggerhead Turtles and Manatees are under serious threat, to name but two. There have been notable success stories, like that of the Bald Eagle whose numbers dropped perilously low in the 1970s but have since recovered through careful conservation. It may be possible for you to become involved with conservation efforts through national or local organizations; if you enjoy wildlife this may be worth considering. Whatever you do, always remember that watching wildlife should always be one thing: enjoyable.

MAMMALS

VIRGINIA OPOSSUM
(DIDELPHIS VIRGINIANA)

Size Length including tail, 22–40 in; weight, 6–14 lb

Description Rat-like, though similar in size to domestic cat. Largely white head; gray, grizzled fur; long, pointed snout; hairless tail and ears

Habitat Woodland, scrubby wasteland and farmlands

Similar species None

The only marsupial – pouched mammal – found in North America: young Virginia Opossums are carried in their mother's pouch for two months after birth. Following this, they ride on their mother's back for a further few weeks. As their teeth develop, their diet changes to incorporate berries, carrion, insects, amphibians, reptiles, small mammals, birds, and their eggs. The Virginia Opossum is an excellent climber, using its prehensile tail to the full. Nocturnal and solitary, it may feign death when threatened (hence the expression "playing possum") or threaten the aggressor in its turn, hissing, screeching, and displaying all its 50 teeth in a wide "grin". It is often unnoticed by humans, though its scavenging behavior can lead to it being found as road kill.

NINE-BANDED ARMADILLO
(DASYPUS NOVEMCINCTUS)

The Nine-banded Armadillo's armor-plating is distinctive; the nine or so narrow, jointed plates covering its midsection make it possible for it to curl into a ball, sometimes doing this when threatened. It digs burrows with its forefeet and nose, and may also burrow if under threat; it can dig with surprising speed and run quickly. It is also able to swim short distances. It searches for insects, which form most of its diet, under leaf litter or vegetation, but also eats carrion and eggs of both birds and reptiles. The female gives birth in a breeding burrow, always to same-sex quadruplets. These are born able to see and can walk shortly after birth; the armor-plating takes longer to develop. It is hunted for both food and the decorative qualities of its shell; it can carry a form of leprosy and has been used in research.

SIZE Length including tail, 25–35 in; weight, 10–15 lb
DESCRIPTION Bony plates covering top of head, body, and tail. Yellow-brown in color; long snout, upright ears, short legs, and long tail
HABITAT Areas with soft soil favored for burrowing; woodland and brushy areas
SIMILAR SPECIES None

STAR-NOSED MOLE
(CONDYLURA CRISTATA)

SIZE Length including tail, 6–8 in; weight, 1–2 oz

DESCRIPTION Large forepaws typical of mole; black, plushy fur; long tail and tentacle-like projections around nose

HABITAT Wet grasslands, woodlands, and swamps

SIMILAR SPECIES Other moles, except for the nose

The Star-nosed Mole's nose, which has a number of sensitive, fleshy, pink projections around the end, easily distinguishes it from other moles. These projections are used to detect the presence of prey, mainly earthworms and snails which it catches in its tunnels. The tunnels are just over an inch in diameter, about 1–2 ft below ground, and frequently end in water. Unlike other moles, the Star-nosed Mole is highly aquatic and catches small crustaceans and fish. This source of food is particularly significant in winter when frozen ground makes burrowing difficult. In addition, the tail is used as a fat reserve: it thickens to provide energy for breeding or times when other sources may be hard to find. Up to 7 young are born in late spring or early summer. Swift developers, they are able to leave the nest after only 3 weeks.

MASKED/CINEREUS SHREW
(SOREX CINEREUS)

Found in a wide variety of habitats, the Masked Shrew is among the most widely distributed shrews. It is more active at night and is not often seen, despite its wide range; it does not hibernate and eats dormant insects during the winter. It constantly searches for food. Like all shrews it has an amazingly high metabolic rate and needs to consume its own body weight in insects, slugs, snails, and worms each day, but even by shrew standards, the Masked Shrew is particularly voracious. It breeds from spring until fall, producing several litters with 5–10 young. These are weaned quickly, within 3 weeks of birth, and few Masked Shrews live longer than a year.

SIZE Length including tail, 3–4 in; weight, $\frac{1}{16}$–$\frac{1}{2}$ oz

DESCRIPTION Small, extremely long-tailed shrew with pointed snout. Gray-brown with silvery underside

HABITAT Prefers damp grasslands, woods, brush and marshes but can be found elsewhere

SIMILAR SPECIES Southeastern Shrew, smaller with a shorter tail; Vagrant Shrew, often lighter in color

(AMERICAN) BEAVER
(CASTOR CANADENSIS)

The Beaver is North America's largest rodent and was threatened with extinction due to fur trapping. It is widespread again and in some areas is even considered a pest. It uses its webbed feet and large tail in swimming; the tail is also slapped on the water surface as an alarm signal. The ears and nose can be closed by valves when diving, and there is also a flap behind the teeth to close the mouth. It can remain submerged for up to 15 minutes at one time. It lives in a burrow by fast-flowing water, but builds dams and lodges in quieter locations, gnawing down trees in a distinctive fashion, leaving stumps with cone-shaped tops. It eats bark and other vegetation, storing food underwater for winter use. The young are born in early summer and the 4–5 "kits" stay with their parents, who usually mate for life, for about two years.

SIZE Length including tail, 3–4½ ft; weight, 30–60+ lb
DESCRIPTION Large aquatic rodent with brown fur, orange teeth, webbed hind feet and a large, flattened tail
HABITAT Inland waters – ponds, lakes, rivers – but slow-moving for preference
SIMILAR SPECIES Muskrats and Nutria are smaller and lack the flat tail

MUSKRAT
(ONDATRA ZIBETHICUS)

SIZE Length including tail, 18–25 in; weight, 2–4 lb

DESCRIPTION Aquatic rodent with red-brown fur and gray belly; partly webbed hind feet and a long, narrow tail

HABITAT Slow-flowing rivers, ponds, lakes, and swamps

SIMILAR SPECIES Both Beaver and Nutria are larger; the Muskrat's tail is flattened laterally (i.e. is higher, not wider)

A closer relative of lemmings and voles rather than beavers, Muskrats do behave similarly to the latter in the construction of their homes. Muskrat lodges are smaller than those of the Beaver, and are built of grasses and sedges rather than the branches of trees. The lodge is usually home to one individual, though it can be shared, except during the breeding season, when they become very territorial and fighting may ensue. The Muskrat generally feeds on aquatic plants, but also sometimes eats snails, crayfish, clams, and frogs; mounds of clam shells are occasionally found at feeding sites. It is an accomplished swimmer and, like the Beaver, the Muskrat is able to remain underwater for periods of time. It breeds prolifically, with several litters produced in a year, and up to 7 young in each litter; the young are independent at about a month old.

BLACK-TAILED PRAIRIE DOG
(CYNOMYS LUDOVICIANUS)

Black-tailed Prairie Dog colonies extended across many miles at one time, but it was thought to compete with cattle for food and numbers were reduced by ranchers. Significant populations remain, however, and the animals continue to live in large groups. Social cohesion is maintained by grooming, touching noses, and a wide range of calls including the barking which has led to this large ground squirrel being called a prairie "dog". Prairie Dog burrows are large and elaborate, the entrances often marked by heaps of earth removed during excavation. These make excellent vantage points and the vegetation around them is often cropped short. The Prairie Dog mainly eats grasses, but also consumes insects like grasshoppers. In spring 4–5 young are born deep in the burrow; they are bald, blind, and deaf and only emerge after 6 weeks. They are fully grown at 6 months.

SIZE Length including tail, 14–16½ in; weight, 2–3 lb

DESCRIPTION Large ground squirrel; yellowish-brown body, paler underside; short, black-tipped tail

HABITAT Shortgrass plains and prairies

SIMILAR SPECIES Other prairie dogs; only this one has a black-tipped tail

WOODCHUCK/ "GROUNDHOG"

(MARMOTA MONAX)

The Woodchuck or Groundhog supposedly emerges from its burrow on February 2, and this has become known as Groundhog Day. However in many areas it does not emerge until later when it is warmer, hibernating deep in the burrow meanwhile. Woodchuck burrows are an extensive system of chambers, tunnels, and multiple openings, and provide excellent insulation. Hibernation usually lasts for 6 months, and the Woodchuck depends upon fat reserves built up the previous summer. It feeds on vegetation like grasses and clover and though it lives on the ground it may evade predators by climbing trees. Mating takes place immediately after hibernation, and this is almost the only time the adults share a burrow. The young are completely helpless at birth, but begin to explore the world outside the burrow after a month. The adult Woodchuck is often seen sitting upright on an entrance mound, scanning the area for danger.

SIZE Length including tail, 18–30 in; weight, 5–12 lb
DESCRIPTION Large rodent with grizzled brown coat, short legs, brown or black feet, and short tail
HABITAT Pastures, meadows, open woodland
SIMILAR SPECIES Within its range, only the Hoary Marmot, which is silvery gray with distinctive facial markings

RED SQUIRREL
(TAMIASCIURUS HUDSONICUS)

SIZE Length including tail, 10–15 in; weight, 5–9 oz

DESCRIPTION Small squirrel with russet-brown fur; white belly; ear tufts in winter

HABITAT Any type of forest

SIMILAR SPECIES Douglas' Squirrel is brown rather than red, and has orange-gray underside

The Red Squirrel is noted for its striking appearance, and is perhaps noisier than other tree-dwelling squirrels with its persistent chatter and a strident, harsh call used to warn of any apparent threat. Active all through the year, the Red Squirrel is especially obvious immediately after sunrise and just before sunset. It has a wide-ranging diet and particularly likes pine cones, which it stores in caches in tree hollows or in the ground; the seeds in the stored cones provide food during the winter. Unlike other squirrels, it doesn't bury individual nuts or acorns. It also eats buds, sap, birds' eggs, and even nestlings, and can happily consume some mushrooms fatal to humans. The Red Squirrel is highly territorial and a female will only permit males on her "patch" when she is receptive; fights are common. Mating is preceded by wild chases, and the litters average 4–5 young.

SOUTHERN FLYING SQUIRREL
(GLAUCOMYS VOLANS)

The Southern Flying Squirrel does not actually fly. The loose skin between fore and hind legs enables it to glide downwards from tree to tree and acts rather like a parachute when it stretches its legs out. To control the glide path, the squirrel uses its tail like a rudder and adjusts its leg position. It is nocturnal, and eats moths and insects, though it also hoards nuts, seeds, and berries for later consumption. It doesn't hibernate as such, but may enter a state of deep sleep when the weather is exceptionally cold or food is scarce. The Southern Flying Squirrel often employs a disused woodpecker hole as a home, but will also use dead trees. In winter several squirrels may share a den; their combined body temperature raises the overall level of warmth. It mates in early spring, and the 2–7 young leave the nest after 5 weeks.

SIZE Length including tail, 8–10 in; weight, 2–3½ oz
DESCRIPTION Small squirrel, gray-brown with white underside; loose skin between front and rear legs
HABITAT Deciduous forests
SIMILAR SPECIES Larger Northern Flying Squirrel prefers coniferous forest; has gray and white underside

THIRTEEN-LINED GROUND SQUIRREL (SPERMOPHILUS TRIDECEMLINEATUS)

SIZE Length including tail, 6½–12 in; weight, 4–9½ oz

DESCRIPTION Pale brown or tan with 13 light and dark stripes alternating on back, partly broken into spots

HABITAT Prairies, parks – wherever grass is kept short

SIMILAR SPECIES Mexican Ground Squirrel, which is larger and lacks the solid stripes

The Thirteen-lined Ground Squirrel is particularly active on sunny, warm days; it remains in its burrow at night and when the weather is unsettled. It hibernates between October and March, living on fat reserves established during the summer. It also stores some food in its burrow which is usually shallow, though it has some deeper chambers for nesting and hibernation. It generally eats plants and seeds but also caterpillars, grasshoppers, and sometimes small mammals like mice and shrews. It often balances on its hind legs to check its immediate surroundings for threats and only rarely goes far from an escape burrow. The Thirteen-lined Ground Squirrel mates in spring and up to 10 young are born in early summer. Often seen on roadsides, it is also, probably inevitably, found as road kill.

EASTERN CHIPMUNK
(TAMIAS STRIATUS)

The Eastern Chipmunk is the only chipmunk in most of eastern North America, and is the largest species. It frequently visits gardens while looking for food, often eating acorns and hickory nuts; it also eats some animals like small snakes, birds, salamanders, slugs, and snails. It stores food in its extensive burrow, eating this during the breaks in hibernation which occur approximately every two weeks throughout the winter. These food stores can be quite large and may even last until the following summer. The Eastern Chipmunk makes two distinctive chattering calls: a rapid chip, chip sound and a lower-pitched chucking noise. It mates in spring and the litter, of 2–8 young, is produced in May. The young Chipmunks are born completely helpless and spend several weeks in the burrow.

SIZE Length including tail, 9–12 in; weight, 2½–5 oz

DESCRIPTION Reddish-brown above with central black stripe and white stripe bordered with black on each side, pale underside; pale facial stripes

HABITAT Deciduous forests, open woodland

SIMILAR SPECIES Least Chipmunk is smaller with more stripes

PLAINS POCKET GOPHER
(GEOMYS BURSARIUS)

SIZE Length including tail, 8–14 in; weight, 5–12½ oz

DESCRIPTION Medium-sized rodent with short, fine brown or black coat, color depending on soil color of habitat; paler underside. Almost naked tail, long claws on front paws

HABITAT Meadows and plains with sandy loam; lawns

SIMILAR SPECIES Only gopher in most of its range; only one with two grooves on outside of upper incisors

Like moles, gophers are rarely seen above ground; their presence is usually revealed by mounds of excavated earth from their extensive tunnel systems. The Plains Pocket Gopher is more active in the summer, when the burrows are also shallower. Like all gophers, it has large, strong claws on the forefeet and prominent incisors which are also used for digging; the eyes and ears are relatively small. It is a herbivore, pulling roots and plant tubers into its tunnels with its teeth, but will also collect plants near the burrow entrance. Any uneaten food is carried in the cheek pouches – the "pockets" which give it its name – and stored in the burrow for later use; it does not hibernate and will rely on these stores when food is scarce. It is a solitary animal, except during the brief mating season in spring; there are usually about 8 in a litter.

NORTH AMERICAN DEER MOUSE
(PEROMYSCUS MANICULATUS)

Deer mice are very variable, live in a variety of habitats and are extremely common. The North American Deer Mouse eats a diverse range of foods: though it is mainly herbivorous, eating fruits, seeds, and nuts, it also eats insects and centipedes. Food is cached for winter use in burrows or hollow logs, and this is transported in the cheek pouches. It is a nocturnal animal, foraging in the dark and resting during daylight in trees, buildings, burrows, and occasionally in birds' nests. It is a significant component of the diet of many predators, especially owls, foxes, and snakes. If there is enough food available the North American Deer Mouse breeds throughout the year, except during the coldest periods, having litters of 5–6 young. It has been associated with both Hanta Virus and Lyme Disease, and close contact should be avoided, both with the animal itself and its droppings.

SIZE Length including tail, 4½–8½ in; weight, 1½–1¼ oz

DESCRIPTION Gray to red-brown above, varying with habitat; white underside, bicolored tail. Woodland and prairie forms exist; woodland is slightly larger

HABITAT Variable and widespread; woodlands, grasslands, brushy areas

SIMILAR SPECIES Can be difficult to distinguish

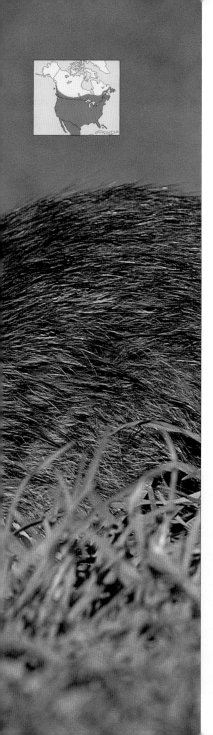

NORWAY RAT/ BROWN RAT
(RATTUS NORVEGICUS)

The Norway Rat was introduced to North America in the late eighteenth century. It has become very successful, exploiting a variety of habitats; it is omnivorous, favoring grain, carrion, insects, and plants but also killing chickens and eating eggs. It has enormous reproductive potential – a female is capable of having up to 12 litters a year, each containing up to 20 young – but food shortages and poor climatic conditions can limit this. Unsurprisingly populations can become seriously overcrowded, at which point migrations may occur. In rural areas it tends to live in burrows; in more urban locations it will choose sewer systems (it is an excellent swimmer) and buildings. It has become a pest, both a public health and economic problem; it contaminates food and spreads communicable diseases which can pose a considerable threat to humans.

Size Length including tail, 12½–18 in; weight, 7 oz–1 lb
Description Brown-gray upper side; gray underside. Scaly tail, slightly less than half total length, paler on underside
Habitat Widespread from farmland to cities
Similar species Black Rat, which has a longer tail

MEADOW VOLE
(MICROTUS PENNSYLVANICUS)

SIZE Length including tail, 5–7½ in; weight, ½–2½ oz

DESCRIPTION Variable color; essentially gray to dark brown, underside paler; tail dark above, pale below

HABITAT Densely vegetated meadows, open woodland, swamps, and marshes

SIMILAR SPECIES Larger than Woodland Vole and many others in its range and habitat; Prairie Vole has shorter tail

The Meadow Vole is mostly active after dark, but is much less so during a full moon; it forms an important part of the diet of many predators, including snakes, owls, and mammals. It does not hibernate but remains active even under snow, safe from the weather in its well-insulated burrow. It is a herbivore, eating grasses, flowers, and roots, and consuming almost the equivalent of its own body weight every day. In the south breeding can occur all year round; in the north this is generally confined to between spring and fall. It builds a spherical nest of grass either along its network of closely cropped pathways or underground in the burrows. There can be population explosions, as the female Meadow Vole is capable of bearing 100 young in a single year, and when this happens there can be considerable damage to crops.

SOUTHERN RED-BACKED VOLE
(CLETHRIONOMYS GAPPERI)

Although the Southern Red-backed Vole has many predators, it is still a common species in many cool, damp habitats, whether woodland or bog. It is often seen running along logs or rocks, across muddy areas, or up tree stumps. It doesn't make its own burrows, but will use those abandoned by other animals. It feeds on berries and green plants, storing less perishable items for use when other food may be scarce; it does not hibernate. Underground fungi are also an important part of its diet. It breeds prolifically, which helps to offset the losses by predation, and female Southern Red-backed Voles can have several litters of up to 8 young in a year. They tend to stay together in family groups until the juveniles get older, at which point the male leaves. Most do not live longer than a year; few will survive two winters.

SIZE Length including tail, 4½–6½ in; weight, ½–1½ oz

DESCRIPTION Small vole, brightly colored, reddish back, yellow-gray flanks and paler underside; short tail

HABITAT Damp woodlands, bogs, swamps, and cool meadows

SIMILAR SPECIES Northern Red-backed Vole has yellower sides and brighter color; Western Red-backed has longer tail. Meadow Vole is larger and not red

MOUNTAIN BEAVER/SEWELLEL/ APLODONTIA (APLODONTIA RUFA)

SIZE Length including tail, 9½–17 in; weight, 1–3 lb

DESCRIPTION Medium-sized rodent with a thick-set body, dark-brown back, paler underside, white spot below ears; very short tail and long claws

HABITAT Damp forests, especially near streams

SIMILAR SPECIES Woodchuck has longer, bushy tail; Muskrat's tail is much longer and scaly

The Mountain Beaver is not exclusively found in mountainous habitats, nor is it a beaver. It does, however, gnaw on bark and collect vegetation but it doesn't build a lodge; this material is piled outside some of the entrances to its burrow. The burrow system is extensive, with numerous openings, and sometimes streams are diverted into the tunnels; these are often close to cover and the Mountain Beaver does not venture far. It is mostly nocturnal but occasionally looks for food in daylight, particularly in fall. It eats vegetation, including some plants most other animals avoid like stinging nettles, and stores food in the burrow for the winter. It can climb trees to reach food, although it is not an accomplished climber. It mates at the end of winter and the litter of 4–5 young is born in early spring. Young Mountain Beavers are not weaned until fall, when they disperse.

PORCUPINE
(ERETHIZON DORSATUM)

The Porcupine is a large nocturnal rodent. An excellent climber, it spends a lot of time in trees and prefers to climb a tree rather than confront an enemy. If necessary, however, it turns its back to the source of danger and chatters. It then gives off a foul odor and, as a last resort, lowers its head, rattles its quills, and strikes out with its tail. The quills detach easily and can become embedded in an attacker, causing serious injury or death. Despite this a few predators have learned to turn them over. The Porcupine feeds on tree leaves, buds and bark, stripping away outer layers, and usually only leaves the trees to move to another source of food or seek shelter. Mating takes place in late fall (the female relaxes her quills to permit mating) and the single young is born in early summer with well-formed but soft quills. Porcupines may live for 7–8 years.

SIZE Length including tail, 25–38 in; weight up to 40 lb

DESCRIPTION Arching body; short legs; front of body covered in long black, brown or yellow hairs; upper rump and tail in long quills

HABITAT Forests, tundra and scrubby land with some trees

SIMILAR SPECIES None

EASTERN COTTONTAIL
(SYLVILAGUS FLORIDANUS)

The Eastern Cottontail is a widespread, common rabbit eastwards of the Rockies. It is a herbivore, eating green vegetation most of the year and woodier stems in winter. It can reingest its droppings which allows it to eat, take cover from predators and then feed again when less vulnerable. It has many predators and few Eastern Cottontails live longer than a year. In winter it may use the burrows of other animals, often Woodchuck, and does not hibernate. Mating can take place any time between late winter and fall, and the breeding season is marked by courtship displays involving males fighting and both sexes jumping dramatically into the air. The female can have several litters a year, each of 1–9 young; she can also mate successfully within hours of giving birth. Litters are born in a depression in the ground lined with vegetation and fur from the mother's breast.

SIZE Length including tail, 15–18 in; weight, 2–4 lb
DESCRIPTION Gray-brown rabbit with reddish nape; long ears; short tail with a white underside
HABITAT Meadows, woodland, brush, lawns, and fields
SIMILAR SPECIES Desert Cottontail is smaller; Swamp Rabbit is larger without the red nape.

AMERICAN PIKA/CONEY
(OCHOTONA PRINCEPS)

SIZE Length, 7–8½ in;
weight, 4–4½ oz

DESCRIPTION Small with
short legs, small rounded
ears and no visible tail.
Gray-brown fur

HABITAT Rocky banks, steep
slopes usually at higher
altitudes (8,000–13,500
ft)

SIMILAR SPECIES Collared
pika has pale band of fur
around neck

Though resembling a rodent, the American Pika is
actually a close relative of rabbits and hares. It lives on
high mountainsides in colonies and communicates by
calling, making a loud bleating sound. The calls echo
deceptively, and may seem to originate from far away
even when the animals are close. The American Pika is a
herbivore, eating many types of green plants including
thistles. It also collects plant material, carrying it to
boulders close to its home and spreading it to dry in the
sun. Piles are often moved to encourage drying or
protect them from rain, and the dry "hay" is stored in
the den among the boulders. It does not hibernate in
winter; its long winter coat keeps it warm and it feeds
on lichens as well as the stored material. It breeds in
spring and a second litter may follow later; 2–6 young
are included in each.

SNOWSHOE HARE
(LEPUS AMERICANUS)

The Snowshoe Hare is sometimes called the "Varying Hare" because it changes color, turning white in winter and reverting to brown in the spring. Initially the white coat is patchy, but by the time the ground is completely covered in snow the hare is also completely covered in white, perfectly camouflaged. It hides during the day among logs, vegetation, or in the deserted burrow of another animal, and is active mainly at night; it has many predators, notably the Lynx. The Snowshoe Hare is essentially a herbivore, feeding on green vegetation in summer and conifer buds and tree bark in winter, but it will also eat carrion. The female can have 2–3 litters in a year, with an average of 3 young in each; they can run almost immediately. Population numbers seem to vary in an approximate ten-year cycle, which can affect predator populations; the reason is not yet established.

SIZE Length including tail, 16–20 in; weight, 2–3 lb

DESCRIPTION Dark brown in summer, white in winter; tail dark above; large ears with black tips

HABITAT Pine forests

SIMILAR SPECIES Smaller than other hares and jackrabbits; Arctic Hare has all-white tail

LITTLE BROWN MYOTIS (MYOTIS LUCIFUGUS)

A common and widely observed bat, females and young Little Brown Myotis form large colonies and roost in buildings during the summer. They move eastwards in fall, hibernating in caves and mines. The male is usually solitary, but roosts with the others in winter. As with many bat species, the Little Brown Myotis mates in fall when moths and other small flying insects are plentiful, but fertilization is delayed: sperm is retained in the female's reproductive tract until spring. During hibernation the Little Brown Myotis wakes frequently and may even leave the roosting site, but it does not feed. A single young is born in early summer, often in a building, and remains in the roost at night while the female hunts. It flies independently at the age of about 4 months.

SIZE Length including tail, 3–3½ in; wingspan, 8–10 in; weight, ⅟₁₆–½ oz

DESCRIPTION Brown glossy fur on back; paler underside; small, round ears

HABITAT Alongside streams and lakes

SIMILAR SPECIES Northern Myotis has longer ears. Most other myotis bats in range have a keeled calcar – the bone from the ankle supporting the tail membrane is bowed outward

MEXICAN/BRAZILIAN FREE-TAILED BAT (BRASILIENSIS TADARIDA)

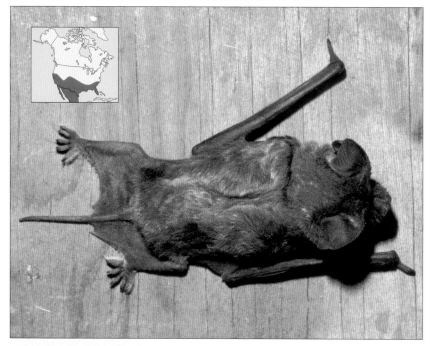

SIZE Length including tail, 3½–4½ in; wingspan, 11 in; weight about ½ oz

DESCRIPTION Dark brown or gray bat, tail extends well beyond edge of interfemoral membrane

HABITAT Varies, includes desert and farmlands

SIMILAR SPECIES Little Free-tailed Bat is similar size but its ears meet at the base

The Brazilian or Mexican Free-tailed Bat occurs throughout Central and South America; it is also found throughout the Southern US. In the eastern parts of its range it hibernates; other populations migrate southwards into Mexico. In Texas, New Mexico, and Arizona these bats live in enormous colonies in caves, packed in at surprising density (250 per sq ft). Just before sunset they begin flittering around the cave and leave shortly after the sun has gone down – the swarms are dramatic and can be seen quitting the caves from some distance away. They feed on insects caught in flight during the night and return to their roost at sunrise. Mating takes place in spring and there is usually a single young, though multiple births of up to 3 are known.

BIG BROWN BAT
(EPTESICUS FUSCUS)

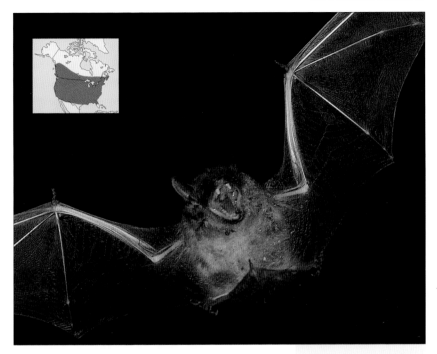

The very common Big Brown Bat is sometimes seen during the day but usually appears at twilight. It is the bat most often seen in winter, sometimes found hibernating in buildings. In winter it roosts alone or with a few others, but spring and summer see the appearance of maternity colonies, which may have several hundred members. In rural areas the Big Brown Bat will often settle in barns or other constructions; it helps farmers by eating pests like June Bugs. It flies quickly, at speeds of 40 mph, and mostly catches beetles and other flying insects; it does not often eat moths or flies. It mates in fall, winter, or spring and produces 2 young. These often tumble to the floor of the maternity roost, but those which manage to clamber up any available structure are often found and retrieved by their mothers, who detect their sharp squeaking.

SIZE Length including tail, 4½–5 in; wingspan, 13 in; weight about ½ oz

DESCRIPTION Large bat, light or dark brown depending on habitat, paler underside. No fur on wings or tail membrane

HABITAT Varied, including forests and urban areas

SIMILAR SPECIES Most other bats in its range are smaller

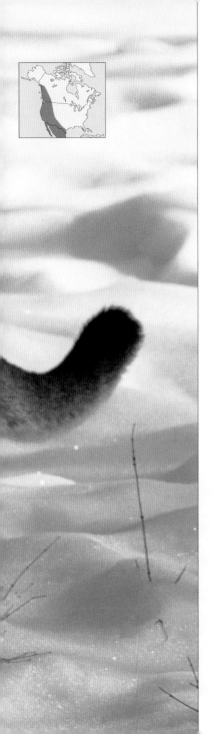

MOUNTAIN LION (PUMA/COUGAR)

(FELIS CONCOLOR)

The Mountain Lion is a solitary and secretive cat, and is seldom seen despite its size and the fact that it sometimes hunts by day. Attacks on humans are rare. It catches deer – an adult can easily bring one down – as well as other mammals and may return to a large kill several times, covering the carcass to hide it between visits. It is an excellent climber and jumper, but rarely swims. The home range is defined by piles of dirt and leaf litter, often scent-marked with urine. The Mountain Lion is extremely vocal, making a variety of calls including blood-curdling screams, growls, and whistles. It usually mates in spring and the young are born in midsummer. Litters vary in size from 1–6 young; between 3–6 months of age these cubs have spotted coats. They stay with their mother for up to two years, becoming increasingly independent.

SIZE Length including tail, 6–8½ ft; weight, 80–270 lb
DESCRIPTION Large brown or tawny yellow unspotted cat; long tail with black tip; dark patches on muzzle sides and ear backs
HABITAT Mountainous areas and forests, swamps
SIMILAR SPECIES None as such; largest native American cat

BOBCAT (LYNX RUFUS)

The Bobcat is generally nocturnal and hides during daylight. It is an expert climber and tends to wait in ambush for suitable prey to pass, rather than tracking it. Though it can kill deer, it usually concentrates on smaller mammals, especially rabbits and hares, and will kill birds and reptiles. If other food is scarce it will eat carrion, often animals killed by human hunters or road kill; in these circumstances it occasionally hunts domesticated animals or poultry. Small animals are eaten immediately but larger prey is hidden and revisited. Vocally, the Bobcat sounds rather like a domestic cat, but it has a piercing scream, particularly yowling during the mating season in early spring; it is a solitary animal except at that time. Young Bobcats are born in litters of 2 or 3 and remain with their mother for a year, perfecting their hunting skills. They are spotted at birth.

Size Length including tail, 2½–4 ft; weight, 15–30 lb
Description Tawny-red to gray-black with darker spots, paler underside; fur on cheeks forms a ruff. Short, barred tail with black tip above, white below
Habitat Scrub, deserts, forests, swamps, cultivated areas
Similar species Lynx has shorter tail with black tip both above and below, and much less distinct spots

(CANADIAN) LYNX
(LYNX CANADENSIS/FELIS LYNX/ LYNX LYNX)

The Lynx is secretive, solitary and primarily nocturnal; it spends the day resting under ledges or fallen trees, or up in the branches. It hunts during the night, either ambushing its prey – often from low branches – or stalking. The Lynx's thick, silky fur and large, fur-covered feet make it perfectly adapted to hunting in snow. The Snowshoe Hare forms a major part of its diet, such an important part, in fact, that Lynx population numbers mirror those of the Snowshoe Hare: when the hares are abundant, more Lynx are born. It will also eat other small mammals, carrion, and deer weakened by bad conditions. A large kill may be hidden and revisited. Lynx only come together during the breeding season in very early spring. Cubs are born 9–10 weeks later, and there may be 1–6 in a litter. Young Lynx stay with their mother for about a year.

SIZE Length including tail, 2½–3½ ft; weight, 12–40 lb
DESCRIPTION Gray cat with blurry darker markings, long ear tufts, large cheek ruffs; short tail with black tip
HABITAT Coniferous forest and swamps
SIMILAR SPECIES Bobcat is browner with more obvious markings and white tip to underside of tail

GRAY WOLF
(CANIS LUPUS)

The Gray Wolf lives in a family pack exhibiting complex social organization, with rigid hierarchies and a single dominant male. They can act more efficiently as a group, making it possible for them to attack large prey such as the Moose. A wolf pack ranges over large distances but will not chase a particular animal for long unless it is showing signs of weakness; prey is more usually ambushed and driven towards the rest of the pack. Large mammals form most of the diet but the Gray Wolf also eats smaller ones and sometimes even berries, fish, and insects. Social bonds are reinforced by a variety of behaviors, including the use of scent and posture, but vocal communication is perhaps the most obvious. Howls are used to keep the pack together, and a wolf may answer a bark by howling. It pairs for life and the 1–11 young, born in a den in spring or early summer, are cared for by the pack. They start to hunt when they are about 4 months old.

SIZE Length including tail, 4½–6½ ft; weight, 60–130 lb
DESCRIPTION Large canine, usually gray grizzled with black, but variable; long, bushy, black-tipped tail
HABITAT Forests and tundra
SIMILAR SPECIES Larger than Red Wolf, Coyote or foxes

COYOTE (CANIS LATRANS)

The Coyote was once almost exclusive to the west, but its range has expanded due to the reduction in range of the Gray Wolf. The Coyote can adapt readily which has aided this expansion, extending even into suburban areas. They sometimes form groups but are normally found alone or in a pair. A Coyote will scavenge, and eats a variety of small animals, insects, fruit, and carrion. It is an efficient swimmer and will pursue its prey into water. Unlike the domestic dog or wolf, it runs with its tail down. Coyotes communicate using a variety of calls, and a long howl followed by barking is the most easily recognizable. Some pair for life; mating takes place in late winter or early spring. Litter sizes vary considerably, from 1–20 young, and they are born in a den which may be an abandoned fox or badger burrow.

SIZE Length including tail, 3½–4½ ft; weight, 20–40 lb
DESCRIPTION Grizzled gray-brown coat, paler belly; bushy, black-tipped tail; large ears
HABITAT Prairies, open woodland or brush; suburbs
SIMILAR SPECIES Gray and Red Wolf are larger; coyote–domestic dog hybrids also tend to be larger with shorter snouts

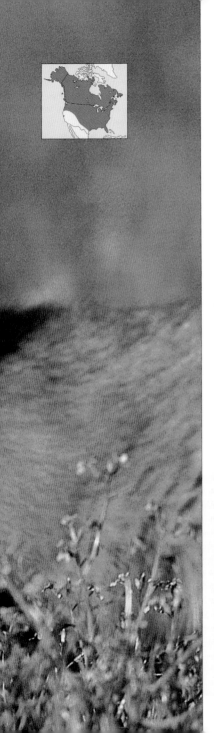

RED FOX
(VULPES VULPES)

Despite being widespread, relatively common, and often living close to humans, the Red Fox is a shy and wary animal and is not frequently seen. It is usually nocturnal but also moves about at dusk and dawn. It is omnivorous; in winter it tends to feed mostly on animals, but its year-round diet includes plenty of vegetation, grasses and berries. It caches food for later use. Red Foxes come together to mate and many pair for life; the breeding season is when they are most vocal. A single litter, of 1–10 young, is born in a den, often a disused burrow of some other animal, in spring or early summer. Initially the cubs are fed on regurgitated food, but their mother soon brings them live prey and begins teaching them how to hunt and kill. They are quickly independent and disperse in the fall.

Size Length including tail, 3–3$\frac{1}{2}$ ft; weight, 8–15 lb
Description Usually rusty red fur, white chin and underside; black legs and feet; bushy tail with white tip
Habitat Varied. Woodland, meadows, cultivated land and suburbs
Similar species The white-tipped tail is distinctive. Common Gray Fox lacks this and has a grayer back

KIT FOX/SWIFT FOX (VULPES VELOX)

SIZE Length including tail, 2–3 ft; weight, 4–6 lb

DESCRIPTION Small with very large ears; sandy-gray fur, white underside; brushy, black-tipped tail

HABITAT Desert and shortgrass prairies

SIMILAR SPECIES Both Red and Gray Foxes are larger

The Kit Fox and the Swift Fox were thought to be separate species, but are now both classified under a single scientific name, Vulpes velox. The Kit Fox is mostly active at night, hunting small animals like squirrels, rabbits, and rats, though it will also eat insects such as crickets; where available, the fruit of cacti also form part of its diet, as do berries and grasses. Males and females come together in late spring for mating and generally pair for life; between 3–5 young are born in a single litter. The birth often takes place in a disused Marmot, Prairie Dog, or American Badger burrow in the spring and family groups stay together until the juveniles become independent. Population numbers have decreased because Kit Foxes have picked up poisoned bait laid down for other species, but they are beginning to recover.

(ALOPEX LAGOPUS) ARCTIC FOX

Like the Snowshoe Hare, the Arctic Fox's color changes mirror the seasons. In winter the molt changes the fur from gray-brown to white, and there is also a rare blue-gray variant in areas without continuous snow cover where a white pelt would be obvious. Its foot pads become furrier, to both protect the feet from cold and make it easier for it to travel in icy conditions. In summer it eats small mammals and some berries; in winter it sometimes tracks Polar Bears in search of carrion. It caches food, either by digging through soil and storing it on the permafrost layer below (thereby freezing it) or hiding it in the rocks. It may travel some distance in search of food. Litter size varies; generally there are 6–12 young born in late spring or summer. Their parents care for them until later in the summer when the family separates.

SIZE Length including tail, 2½–3 ft; weight, 6–9 lb

DESCRIPTION Small, short legs, rounded ears; color varies from gray-brown in summer to white in winter

HABITAT Northern forest edges, tundra, ice floes

SIMILAR SPECIES Only the quite different Red Fox shares its range

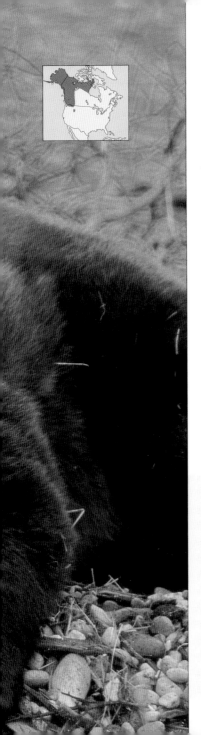

GRIZZLY/ BROWN BEAR
(URSUS ARCTOS)

Powerful, large, and often unpredictable, the Grizzly Bear is possibly the most dangerous bear in North America. It avoids human contact, except in areas where it has become accustomed to the presence of people, and can pose a threat if surprised or with young. It is usually more active at night. It can move at speed over short distances, and the cubs can climb. Omnivorous, it eats plant roots and shoots, fungi, leaves, fish, insects, mammals of all sizes, and carrion. It digs insects out of rotting wood, will claw small animals from their burrows, and is a skilled fisher. Salmon migrations can attract simultaneous attention from numbers of bears, and fights can break out among these normally solitary animals. It puts on fat reserves for winter and "dens up" in a cave or similar safe place; it can, however, be easily woken. It mates in summer and the litter of 1–4 cubs is born in late winter or spring. At birth the cubs are tiny, only about a pound in weight.

SIZE Length including tail, 6–7 ft; weight, 300–1000 lb
DESCRIPTION Light to dark brown fur, frequently grizzled with white-tipped hairs; shoulder hump; long front claws
HABITAT Mountainous grasslands, forests, tundra
SIMILAR SPECIES Black Bear is smaller, lacks shoulder hump

BLACK BEAR
(URSUS AMERICANUS)

The Black Bear can be dangerous to people, becoming a problem in places where it has discovered the advantages of garbage dumps. Most of its diet is of vegetable origin – roots, buds, leaves, the inner bark of trees, berries, and nuts – though it will tear rotten wood apart to reach insects and has been known to demolish beehives searching for honey. It is an excellent fisher and also eats smaller mammals. During fall it accumulates a layer of fat and holes up for the worst of the winter. Essentially a solitary animal, Black Bears only really come together for mating, though they may congregate around dumps at any time. Mating occurs during the summer and a female only has a single cub in her first breeding year; after that 2 are the norm. Black Bear cubs are very small, weighing only 7 oz, and they may nurse for up to a year, during which time the mother is not receptive to males.

SIZE Length including tail, $4\frac{1}{2}$–6 ft; weight, 200–550 lb
DESCRIPTION Color varies geographically; eastern bears almost black and western ones brown, cinnamon or even blond; paler snout
HABITAT Forest, swamps, mountainous woodland
SIMILAR SPECIES Grizzly Bear is larger and has shoulder hump

POLAR BEAR
(URSUS MARITIMUS)

The Polar Bear can be active throughout the day and year, hunting for fish, seals, and young walrus. It also eats carrion, birds, shellfish, and even mushrooms and algae. Though a powerful swimmer, it is not swift enough to catch seals in the water: it stalks or ambushes them on the ice or when they come up to their breathing holes. It has a sharp sense of smell and can locate prey by scent below ice or snowdrifts. During the worst of the winter it may hole up in a den excavated in the snow. Pregnant females stay in the den for several months, during which time they will give birth; cubs are usually born in alternate years. Other Polar Bears den up for a shorter length of time, though they may leave at any point. Cubs are born between November and January, and stay with their mother for well over a year. Like all bears, it can be unpredictable.

SIZE Length including tail, 7–11 ft; weight, 700–1200 lb
DESCRIPTION White or yellowish-white fur; long neck and legs; relatively small head and ears
HABITAT Coastlines, pack ice, ice floes
SIMILAR SPECIES None

COMMON/NORTHERN RACCOON (PROCYON LOTOR)

SIZE Length including tail, 2–3 ft; weight, 12–45 lb

DESCRIPTION Gray or reddish-brown with black flecks; black mask around eyes edge in white; bushy tail with black rings

HABITAT Woodlands, wetlands; rural, urban, and suburban areas

SIMILAR SPECIES Ringtail and White-nosed Coati are smaller; Ringtail has no mask

Highly adaptable, the Common Raccoon lives in a wide variety of habitats and has no fear of humans. It can climb and swim well. It does not truly hibernate, though it may be inactive for periods of time and builds up fat reserves during fall. Omnivorous, it will even open refrigerators and lift the lids from garbage cans. In rural habitats it is commonly found close to water where it catches fish, insects, amphibians, and reptiles; though it seems to wash this food, it actually breaks it up in the water. It mates in winter or early spring; there are 1–8 young in a litter which is born in a den or safe place such as a culvert. They are weaned by late summer; some leave in fall and others may stay with their mother until she drives them away before the birth of the next litter.

NORTHERN RIVER OTTER
(LUTRA CANADENSIS)

Mainly nocturnal, the Northern River Otter may sometimes be seen in daylight. Otters are sociable and noted for their evident enjoyment of play, sliding down slopes, chasing each other, rolling about. Even when alone it seems an otter has fun, tumbling about or body-surfing on fast-flowing water. Agile on land, it is superb in the water, a swift and powerful hunter of frequently large fish. It can stay underwater for several minutes at a time. Its diet mainly consists of fish but it will also eat frogs, crayfish, and small animals; aquatic prey is carried to the bank to be eaten. A permanent den may be excavated on a riverbank and the otter mates in spring, just after the birth of a litter. Implantation is delayed, and the 1–6 young are born the next March or April. The juveniles disperse in the early spring.

SIZE Length including tail, 3–4 ft; weight, 12–30 lb

DESCRIPTION Streamlined body with long tail, short legs, webbed feet; dark brown coat, paler on throat

HABITAT Lakes, rivers, marshes, occasionally coastal areas

SIMILAR SPECIES Sea Otter is larger and found in salt water along parts of Pacific coast

SEA OTTER (ENHYDRA LUTRIS)

SIZE Length including tail,
3–5½ ft; weight, 25–75 lb

DESCRIPTION Dark brown, gray
underside and head; short tail
and webbed feet; hind feet
are flipper-like

HABITAT Coastal waters, kelp
beds along Pacific coast

SIMILAR SPECIES The smaller
Northern River Otter is not
found in salt water

The Sea Otter is highly aquatic, hardly ever coming
ashore, though rarely going far out to sea. Its food –
abalone, sea urchins, crabs, fish, mussels – is most
abundant in coastal shallows. It feeds, sleeps and
gives birth at sea; despite this it is not an agile
swimmer. It is often seen floating on its back. It has
no blubber and relies on the insulating qualities of its
fur, so grooming is an important activity. The Sea
Otter is among the very few animals to use tools. It
picks up a stone when diving for food then floats on
its back, the stone on its chest, and cracks shells
against it. It is sociable, and this extends to other
species such as seals and sea lions. A single young is
born in winter or spring; the pup is weaned at a year
but may stay with the mother even after the birth of
the next pup.

(MUSTELA VISON) MINK

The Mink is a determined predator; semi-aquatic, it hunts for fish but also for a wide variety of prey including waterfowl and mammals like muskrats which form an important part of the diet. It kills by biting the neck and eats at the kill site, though it may drag prey back to the den which is always near water, generally a disused burrow of another species, and temporary. It is an excellent swimmer, with partly webbed feet, and can dive to more than 16 ft. Highly territorial, it fights whenever it encounters other mink except during breeding. It scent-marks its territory with a foul-smelling discharge from its anal glands which it also uses if threatened. Mating occurs between late winter and April; up to 10 young are born in a den and are weaned at about 6 weeks. The family separates in early fall.

SIZE Length including tail, 18–28 in; weight, 2–3½ lb

DESCRIPTION Long, streamlined body; dark brown or black, small white patch on chin; long, bushy tail

HABITAT Near fresh water, rivers, lakes, streams, marshes

SIMILAR SPECIES American Marten has longer tail, buff or orange throat

AMERICAN MARTEN (MARTES AMERICANA)

SIZE Length including tail, 20–27 in; weight, 1½–3½ lb

DESCRIPTION Long and slender; brown back, lighter face and underside, orange or buff throat patch; long, bushy tail

HABITAT Mainly coniferous forests

SIMILAR SPECIES Mink is darker and has distinctive white chin; Fisher is much larger

Mainly nocturnal, the American Marten is a good climber and often uses a hollow tree, squirrel nest, or woodpecker hole as a daytime refuge. During the night, dawn, dusk, or overcast weather it hunts rodents on the ground. Red-backed Voles are an important component of the diet, but it also eats rabbits, squirrels, carrion, insects, earthworms, berries, and honey. It is usually solitary and behaves aggressively if it meets another, snarling and growling; it makes a variety of other noises including screams, chuckles, and whines. Both sexes scent-mark logs and branches, dragging the scent glands on the abdomen over the surface. Martens mate in midsummer but implantation is delayed until midwinter. A litter of on average 3–4 helpless young is born in late spring; they are weaned 6 weeks later.

(TAXIDEA TAXUS) AMERICAN BADGER

The American Badger is squat and powerful, with strong claws for digging. Generally nocturnal, daylight is spent in a burrow. A single badger may have several such dens in its territory, moving between them while searching for food. The burrow has a single entrance and a latrine area may be located just outside; the entrance can be blocked during severe weather. The American Badger eats a variety of small mammals but is particularly suited to catching ones that also burrow, like Prairie Dogs, which it digs out. Excess food is stored. It can be very aggressive and has few predators, but usually prefers to retreat rather than fight. American Badgers only come together during the mating season in late summer; implantation is delayed and up to 5 young are born in a maternal den in spring. They disperse in late summer.

SIZE Length including tail, 2–2½ ft; weight, 8–25 lbs

DESCRIPTION Broad; gray shaggy fur, distinctive facial markings including white stripe running over the head to the nape or further; short legs

HABITAT Open grasslands, prairies, farmlands, sometimes near woods

SIMILAR SPECIES Wolverine is larger and lacks typical facial markings

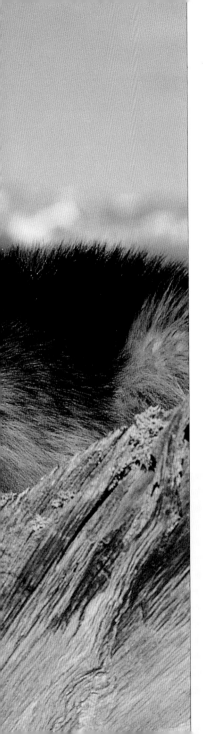

WOLVERINE

(GULO GULO)

The male Wolverine has an enormous home range of more than 1000 square miles through which it moves constantly, searching for food. It is powerful and omnivorous, and one of its popular names is the "Glutton": it eats anything it can find from Moose slowed by snow to vegetation. It is so aggressive that it is capable of driving other predators, even Mountain Lions and bears, away from a kill. The Wolverine scent-marks any excess food with a foul-smelling musk which other scavengers evidently find repulsive. Its den is in a protected place such as a crevice. The mating season is extended, possibly to increase the likelihood of the sexes encountering each other. It does not hibernate, but implantation is delayed and the litter of 2–5 young is born in early spring. Juvenile Wolverines remain with their mother for 2 years.

SIZE Length including tail, 3–3½ ft; weight, 20–40 lbs
DESCRIPTION Heavily built, short legs, fairly short tail; dark brown coat with yellowish bands from shoulder to tail; lighter above the eyes
HABITAT High mountains, tundra
SIMILAR SPECIES American Badger has somewhat similar build but different markings

LONG-TAILED WEASEL (MUSTELA FRENATA)

SIZE Length including tail, 11-20 in; weight, 4–11 oz

DESCRIPTION Long, slim body; brown, paler underside; tail with black tip

HABITAT Varies; usually near water, open country

SIMILAR SPECIES Short-tailed Weasel is smaller and has white feet; Black-footed Ferret is yellow-brown with dark eye mask

A voracious carnivore, the Long-tailed Weasel is widespread, preying mainly on mice and voles but capable of tackling prey larger than itself if nothing smaller is available. It helps to control rabbits, but hunts birds and can do serious damage in a chicken coop. Weasels sometimes indulge in a killing spree; their instinct is to kill when food is available and store it. It is a prey animal itself; when threatened it releases a foul musk from its anal glands which it also uses for scent-marking. It dens in other animals' disused burrows, constructing an inner nest. It mates in summer but final implantation is delayed until spring. There are 4–8 young in the litter, born blind and almost naked. They mature quickly, however, and separate from their mother after about 2 months. In more northerly areas the Long-tailed Weasel turns white during the pre-winter molt; it retains the black tail tip.

(MEPHITIS MEPHITIS) STRIPED SKUNK

The Striped Skunk's coloring acts as a warning that it is best avoided; if not, it releases a fetid, stinking musk from its anal glands. It does not usually need to do this, as its initial display is enough to persuade many predators to retreat. Should they fail to do so, the skunk will turn its back, raise its tail, and spray. The smell can be detected for a mile. Omnivorous, the Striped Skunk is essentially nocturnal and will consume anything appropriate to its size, eating a lot in fall to prepare for winter though it does not hibernate. It dens in an abandoned burrow, though it will sometimes dig its own; maternal dens are always underground. It mates in spring, and the litter of 4–7 young is born in May or June; they carry the distinctive markings from birth. Striped Skunks are the main carriers of rabies in the US.

SIZE Length including tail, 20–30 in; weight, 7–15 lbs

DESCRIPTION Black with 2 white stripes on back, meeting at neck and base of bushy tail; latter tipped and fringed in white; white facial stripe

HABITAT Desert, grassy plains, woodlands, suburbs

SIMILAR SPECIES Common Hog-nosed Skunk has white back and tail; Hooded Skunk is usually mostly black with narrow white stripes

COLLARED PECCARY (TAYASSU TAJACU)

SIZE Length including tail, 3–3½ ft; weight, 30–60 lb

DESCRIPTION Large head with long snout and small tusks; grizzled gray or black coat with white shoulder collar; inconspicuous tail

HABITAT Brushy desert, rocky areas

SIMILAR SPECIES Feral Pig much larger, as is Wild Boar

The Collared Peccary is the only pig-like animal native to North America. It is subtropical and is only found in some southern States; originally its range extended further north but it was hunted for both meat and hide. Herds were once enormous; today they consist of 6–30 animals. Led by a dominant male, a group is strongly territorial. Though stable, sub-groups may form and detach themselves temporarily in order to feed. The Collared Peccary secretes a strong cheesy musk which may help unite group members; it certainly acts as an involuntary alarm signal. A herbivore most of the time, it occasionally eats insects, reptiles and small mammals. It can breed throughout the year but many young peccaries are born in summer. One litter, of 2–6 young, is produced each year, although a second may follow if the first does not survive.

(OVIS CANADENSIS) BIGHORN SHEEP

The Bighorn Sheep is a good swimmer and remarkable climber; the hooves have soft soles enabling it to cross precipitous terrain. Most of its time is spent on high mountain slopes and it sleeps in a scrape or depression wherever it happens to be, often on ridges but sometimes in caves. It eats vegetation, migrating between higher slopes in summer and high valleys in winter. Bighorn Sheep live in small, sex-segregated bands: small ram bands and larger ones led by an old ewe. They join in winter when there can be 100 individuals in a herd, all led by the matriarch. In fall the rams begin butting contests, charging each other at speed, and the dominant ram does most of the mating. A single lamb is born in early summer; lambing takes place in the most inaccessible areas. Unsurprisingly the lamb is well-developed; it can walk and climb almost immediately.

SIZE Length including tail, 4½–6 ft; weight, 80–300 lb

DESCRIPTION Brown sheep; white nose, underparts, rump patch; large spiral horns in male; female's horns smaller and less curved

HABITAT Rocky slopes, cliffs, canyons with scattered vegetation

SIMILAR SPECIES None within its range

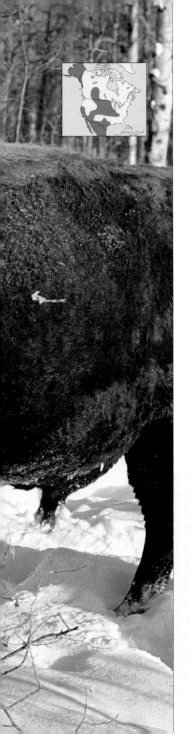

(AMERICAN) BISON/ BUFFALO (BISON BISON)

The American Bison or Buffalo is the largest land animal in North America. Millions once grazed the plains and were central to the life of Native Americans. The deliberate destruction of the species took place in the nineteenth century. Efforts to preserve them started early in the twentieth; it survives mainly in National Parks and private ranches. At its most active at cooler times of day, it eats grass and other vegetation, if necessary clearing winter snow with its hooves and head. Outside of the breeding season the sexes form separate herds, often quite small; during breeding the herds combine, increasing in size. As bulls age they become more solitary. During the breeding season – between June and September – they become aggressive and may fight each other. Following mating, and a gestation period of about 9 months, a single calf is usually born, though there are sometimes twins. Calves can stand and walk very quickly; with their mothers they may form a nursery herd.

SIZE Length including tail, 7–12½ ft; weight, 800-1200 lb
DESCRIPTION Huge, males up to 6 ft tall at shoulder, which is humped; dark brown, shaggy mane over forequarters extends down front legs; massive head, relatively short black horns
HABITAT Varied; prairie, plains, sometimes woodland
SIMILAR SPECIES None

MOOSE (ALCES ALCES)

The Moose is essentially solitary but may form small groups to exploit good food sources. The male is particularly distinctive; the antlers start developing in spring, are at their largest in late summer, and are shed in winter. It feeds on aquatic vegetation and on woody plants in winter. The mating season comes in fall and can be noisy, the males "barking" and bellowing, challenging rivals as they charge through the forest seeking females. Mock fights and challenges occur between males and can escalate into actual fights which may be fatal; this is usually avoided as one male will often back down. Calves, usually 1 or 2, are born in early summer, can walk quickly and swim within 2 weeks. They are driven away by their mothers just before the birth of the next calf.

SIZE Length including tail, 7–10 ft; weight, 700–1400 lb

DESCRIPTION Dark brown, paler legs; shoulder hump, huge head with pendulous muzzle. Males' flattened antlers can be 5 ft across; the hanging dewlap is unique

HABITAT Forests, especially in marshy regions

SIMILAR SPECIES Distinguished from other deer by size, nose shape and antlers

ELK/WAPITI
(CERVUS ELAPHUS)

The Elk, also known by the Shawnee name of Wapiti, is highly sociable and herds can have hundreds of members. Most are cows and calves, the bulls tending to group together on the edges. The Elk feeds on many kinds of vegetation, usually grazing, but will also eat lichen. The amount and quality of available food seems to be a determining factor in the time of mating, the number of cows who conceive, and the age of puberty. During breeding males may "joust", clashing their antlers, but they are not often injured. They also make distinctive bugling calls, roll in stagnant water or mud, and toss scent-marked grasses over their backs. A single bull herds many cows together and may mate with as many as 50, establishing a harem. Calves, born after 9 months, join a nursery herd for the first few weeks; then the cows and calves herd together.

SIZE Length including tail, 7–10 ft; weight, 500–1000 lb

DESCRIPTION Brown with pale rump, yellowish tail, grayer in winter; males have large branching antlers summer through spring

HABITAT Mountainous woodlands, pastures, lake shores

SIMILAR SPECIES Bigger than other deer except Moose, which has flattened antlers, larger muzzle and dewlap

WHITE-TAILED DEER
(ODOCOILEUS VIRGINIANUS)

The White-tailed Deer is common, widespread, and generally nocturnal, though it may be active at any time of day. In summer it feeds on green plants, with nuts entering the diet in fall and woody vegetation becoming important in winter. It often uses distinct trails to reach feeding areas; the group then spreads out to feed. This group may consist of a doe and her fawns; bucks form a separate band. The male bands are stable, sociable groups until the breeding season when they begin to challenge each other for dominance; two males will spar, trying to push each other into reversing. Larger, matriarchal but mixed-sex groups may form in winter, with over 100 members. A doe's first offspring is usually a single fawn; thereafter twins or even triplets are common. They usually stay with their mother until the next are born, at which point she drives the older ones away.

SIZE Length including tail, 4½–7 ft; weight, 90–300 lb
DESCRIPTION Red-brown or tan above, grayer in winter; underside, throat, tail edges white. Males antlers spread to around 3 ft
HABITAT Woodlands, farmlands, brush, suburbs
SIMILAR SPECIES Mule Deer has tail tipped with black

PRONGHORN (ANTILOCAPRA AMERICANA)

SIZE Length including tail, 4–4½ ft; weight, 80–130 lb
DESCRIPTION Deer-like, long legs; tan with white on rump and belly, two white stripes on throat; distinctive black horns
HABITAT Grasslands, prairie, brush
SIMILAR SPECIES None

The Pronghorn has been recorded running at 70 mph for minutes at a time; speeds of 45 mph are not uncommon. When running it keeps its mouth open to maximize oxygen intake. It feeds on a variety of plants, including cacti, and does not drink much if it can eat green vegetation. It can reach food through light snow cover, but worse weather forces it to migrate. There were once large herds across the prairies but numbers were much reduced; its range is expanding once more in response to conservation measures. During summer it roams in scattered groups with older males separate from the females, fawns and younger males. The experienced males establish territories and defend them against challengers. The Pronghorn mates in early fall and fawns are born in early summer. Fawns have virtually no odor to minimize the risk of predation; in addition, the female will separate twins.

(CALLORHINUS URSINUS) NORTHERN FUR SEAL

The Northern Fur Seal is solitary, coming ashore and coming together only to breed. It hunts fish and squid, but also birds and other marine mammals. The Pribilof Islands are its main breeding area and over a million may gather there in summer. Older bulls arrive in late May or early June, and establish their territories before the females appear. They try to herd the females into harems, guarding them from other males, often aggressively. Females give birth almost immediately to a calf conceived the previous year. This is suckled for about a week; the female then mates and begins to go on feeding trips, returning to nurse her young. Males do not feed during breeding, and may be weak from hunger and fighting when they return to the water in August as the season ends. Year-old males and females come ashore to mate in late summer, and all disperse by fall.

SIZE Length, 3½–7 ft; weight, 85–600 lbs

DESCRIPTION Eared seal; large flippers, tiny tail, small head; blackish above, reddish below. Male larger than female

HABITAT Cold seas most of year; breeding in summer on rocky beaches

SIMILAR SPECIES Northern Elephant Seal and Sea Lions are larger; Harbor Seal is spotted

COMMON/HARBOR SEAL
(PHOCA VITULINA)

SIZE Length, 4–6 ft; weight, 150–300 lbs

DESCRIPTION Varying in color, pale gray, yellowish-gray, or brownish with dark spots; or black, brown, or gray with light rings. Male larger than female

HABITAT Coastal waters, estuaries, harbors, occasionally lakes

SIMILAR SPECIES Spotted Seal, but on pack ice; Gray Seal often spotted but with less dog-like face; young very alike

As do most seals, the Harbor Seal generally eats fish, mollusks, and crustaceans; some steal fish from nets. In spring it may follow spawning fish up rivers and there are some living exclusively in freshwater lakes. Harbor Seals are extremely sociable and can often be seen in groups basking on beaches at low tide, returning to the water as the tide comes back in. These groups can sometimes be very large, occasionally numbering thousands of individuals. The breeding season varies, with females bearing a single pup any time between late spring and late summer, normally in the intertidal zone, in places like sandbars. The young Harbor Seal swims with its mother very soon after birth, unlike most seal pups which stay on land at first; it may ride on her back as she submerges.

NORTHERN ELEPHANT SEAL
(MIROUNGA ANGUSTIROSTRIS)

Despite its bulk, the Northern Elephant Seal is the world's second-largest seal: it is smaller than the Southern Elephant Seal which lives in the Antarctic. The Northern Elephant Seal feeds on deep-sea fish and squid, and can remain underwater for over an hour, feeding as deep as 5000 ft. It breeds on sandy beaches; the bulls arrive in about December. Contests for territory then take place, with the huge bulls bellowing and inflating their noses. If this display is insufficient, they lunge at each other with their teeth; most mature males are heavily scarred. By the time the females arrive the majority of territories have been established. A single pup, which can weigh 80 lb, is born about a week after the female's arrival. Once it is weaned, mating takes place and the female returns to the sea. Northern Elephant Seals return to the beaches to molt in late May; the weaned young have remained there, living off their fat and practicing swimming.

SIZE Length, 10–15½ ft; weight, 1000–1400 lb

DESCRIPTION Enormous, brown or gray; large, rounded head. Males much larger than females, developing thick, trunk-like nose by adulthood

HABITAT Open ocean, temperate seas, sandy beaches for breeding

SIMILAR SPECIES None

CALIFORNIA SEA LION
(ZALOPHUS CALIFORNIANUS)

Playful, swift, and curious in the wild, the California Sea Lion can often be seen throwing objects, including large fish, clear of the sea and catching them on its nose. It can be too inquisitive: many become fatally entangled in nets or caught in debris. It swims at speeds of up to 40 mph, and hunts for prey including squid and over 50 types of fish. Days are spent ashore, basking. Sociable, the California Sea Lion often forms groups separated by sex outside of the breeding season. Males bark while defending territories; females wail to summon pups, and growl and bark with other females; pups bleat. The males noisily establish breeding territories on beaches in May or June, fighting if necessary; the females arrive to give birth around the same time. About 3–4 weeks after the birth of a single pup the female mates. The males leave the breeding colonies in late summer or early fall.

SIZE Length, 5–8 ft; weight, 100–850 lb
DESCRIPTION Slender, brownish fur appearing black when wet; high forehead, small ears; frequent barking. Males are larger than females
HABITAT Open sea, surf, rocky coasts, rocky or sandy beaches
SIMILAR SPECIES Northern Sea Lion is larger and paler

WALRUS
(ODOBENUS ROSMARUS)

Walruses are extremely sociable and congregate in large mixed-sex herds which sometimes segregate by sex outside of the breeding season; if any Walrus is attacked, adult or juvenile, its neighbors will come to its aid. It spends a lot of time on land, rotating its hind flippers to enable it to walk. A bottom feeder, it forages for mollusks, particularly clams, using the sensitive whiskers to detect them in the sand; they are dislodged using the tusks. A few fish, shrimp, and worms are additions to the diet and males will sometimes attack seals, grabbing and then stabbing with the tusks. Tusks are also used in self-defense and during the breeding season in disputes with other males. Mating takes place in late winter, and a single calf is born the following spring or summer; the female does not breed in the year she gives birth. A young Walrus stays with its mother until its tusks have developed; usually about 2 years. A female will even defend her calf from a Polar Bear.

SIZE Length, 7½–12 ft; weight, 800–3000+ lb
DESCRIPTION Pink or brownish body, bristled muzzle, large tusks. Males larger than females, individuals from Pacific also larger
HABITAT Shallower waters around pack ice
SIMILAR SPECIES None

(WEST INDIAN) MANATEE
(TRICHECHUS MANATUS)

The Manatee is generally nocturnal, feeding on aquatic plants like water hyacinth. It never leaves the water completely, though it has been known to graze on bankside vegetation, even eating acorns. Found exclusively in warmer waters, it is sometimes attracted to power station outflows despite there being less food. Manatees gather in small groups and there is no fixed breeding season; females produce young every two or three years, probably when conditions are at their most favorable. There is a long gestation period of up to 14 months and the single calf is nursed underwater. It starts eating vegetation a few weeks into weaning, but may stay with its mother for as long as two years. Manatees are more closely related to elephants than to other marine mammals. They were once hunted and are now an endangered species: human activity can destroy habitats and boat propellers present a danger.

SIZE Length including tail, 8–12 ft; weight, 1000–3500 lb
DESCRIPTION Huge body, grayish or blackish when wet; forelegs adapted into paddles, hind legs into a single fluke
HABITAT Shallow coastal waters, estuaries, rivers, lagoons
SIMILAR SPECIES None

BIRDS

COMMON LOON
(GAVIA IMMER)

SIZE Length, 2½ ft

DESCRIPTION Thick neck and bill; dark plumage with white checker-patterned back in summer

HABITAT Forest lakes, coastal areas

SIMILAR SPECIES Like other loons in winter, but with larger head; Yellow-billed Loon resembles it in summer but is larger, heavier, and has bright yellow bill

A medium-sized seabird, the Common Loon's breeding season plumage – extensive back-and-white checker pattern, black-and-white collar, and "chin strap" – is distinctive, as are its yodeling calls. It is relatively common across the northern US and Canada in summer, but population numbers are declining due to habitat destruction and pollution. Breeding and nesting both take place on large bodies of water. The Common Loon migrates in order to winter on both eastern and western coasts, or on any ice-free lake. Migrating Common Loons generally fly higher than any other members of the loon family, and move both overland and along the coasts. It can also dive for more than 150 ft while searching for fish, and may stay underwater for long periods.

AMERICAN WHITE PELICAN
(PELECANUS ERYTHRORHYNCHOS)

A large, sturdy bird with a huge wingspan, the American White Pelican is awkward on land but impressive when flying. It is often found in flocks and nests near the water. The pelicans may also hunt in flocks, searching for fish which are caught in the bill. This, together with the throat pouch which is filled as the bird swims, can hold nearly 3 gallons – more than double the stomach capacity. Hunting flocks sometimes form a line, driving fish into shallows from which they cannot escape. Two eggs are laid on a large nest mound, and the chicks are naked when they hatch; they are protected from the sun by a parent. In the breeding season adult birds develop a fibrous plate on the upper mandible of the bill, together with a yellowish crest, but both vanish once the eggs are produced. Juvenile birds have brownish heads, necks, and backs.

SIZE Length, 5 ft; wingspan, 9 ft
DESCRIPTION large; white plumage, black on trailing edge of wings; large, yellow pouched bill
HABITAT Seawater, lakes
SIMILAR SPECIES Almost unmistakable; wing pattern in flight similar to Wood Stork

DOUBLE-CRESTED CORMORANT
(PHALACROCORAX AURITUS)

The Double-crested Cormorant is the only North American cormorant to be found on both east and west coasts, and is also the most widespread. Any cormorant seen on a lake will almost certainly be a Double-crested. It dives and swims underwater when hunting for fish and swims on the surface rather low in the water, a little like a loon. The flight formation is a V shape, rather like that of geese. During the breeding season the adult develops small tufts on the side of the head which are whitish in northern and western populations, and black in those from the southeast. Nesting colonies may be located on rocky islands, cliff edges, or high up in trees, but are always near deep water. The nest is a mound of seaweed or sticks and the 2–9 eggs are incubated for just over 3 weeks by both parents.

Size Length, 2½ ft; wingspan, 4 ft
Description Hook-tipped bill; black plumage, orange-yellow throat pouch, head tufts in breeding season. In flight head held in a kink
Habitat Seawater, inland lakes and rivers
Similar species Great Cormorant has similar plumage but is larger; Brandt's Cormorant lacks the colored throat patch

GREAT BLUE HERON
(ARDEA HERODIAS)

The Great Blue Heron is the largest heron in North America and the most widespread. A lone Great Blue is often seen flying along, slow and stately. It flies up to 10–15 miles in search of a feeding ground where there are plenty of fish, and waits patiently, standing on the bank before it spears its catch. Fish form the major part of the diet, but it will also eat small mammals, frogs, and snakes. Though generally solitary, it tends to nest in large colonies. The nest is built high off the ground in trees or on cliffs and is a messy heap of sticks. The 3–7 eggs are incubated by both birds for about a month, and the chicks leave the nest after a further 8 weeks. Juvenile birds are grayer-brown in color and lack plumes. The all-white version found in Florida was previously thought to be another species.

SIZE Length, 4 ft; wingspan, 6 ft
DESCRIPTION Long legs and neck; plumage gray-blue, white head with black stripe ending in plumes behind the eye; spear-like bill
HABITAT Wetlands, still water
SIMILAR SPECIES Size distinguishes it; all-white form is similar to Great Egret but larger

GREAT EGRET (ARDEA ALBA)

SIZE Length, 3 ft; wingspan, 4 ft

DESCRIPTION Large, long neck and legs; white with black legs; long, thin yellow bill; breeding birds have long plumes extending from their back to beyond the tail

HABITAT Lakes, marshes, wetlands

SIMILAR SPECIES Most other white herons are smaller; black legs distinguish it from all-white variety of Great Blue Heron

The population of Great Egrets was much diminished in the nineteenth century by hunters killing them for their beautiful feathers. Though it is the most widespread egret in North America it is not out of danger today, with drainage of wetlands restricting available habitats. The Great Egret can be seen elegantly walking in shallow water, stalking fish, frogs, and water snakes; it also eats insects. A sociable bird, it is a colonial nester, and Great Egret colonies can be large. Nests are generally built in trees but may be found in reeds, and are sturdy, reusable platforms constructed with sticks. Here 3–5 eggs are laid; both adult birds incubate the clutch for 23–36 days, and the chicks stay in the nest for a further 6–7 weeks. Juvenile birds are white, but not of such an almost luminous brightness as adults; they have no plumes.

(CYGNUS COLUMBIANUS) TUNDRA SWAN

As its name suggests, the Tundra Swan – formerly known as the Whistling Swan because of its musical voice – is principally found on the Arctic tundra. It is the smallest North American swan, spending summers in the north but migrating southwards in winter. It is often seen in flocks and has a tendency to return to the same place year after year. Most Tundra Swans feed on both land and water; they eat small mollusks, invertebrates, and aquatic plants. Breeding takes place on the tundra, where it builds a large mound of grass and leaves as its nest; the 2–7 eggs are incubated by the female for an average of 32 days. A young Tundra Swan has gray-brown plumage and appears rather dull; its bill is pink. It develops its adult coloration more quickly than do juveniles of other swan species.

SIZE Length, 4½ ft; wingspan, 6½ ft

DESCRIPTION Large, long neck; white with black bill, bright yellow spot in front of eye; neck generally held straight

HABITAT Shallow ponds, lakes, marshes, rivers

SIMILAR SPECIES Trumpeter Swan has longer bill and is larger, as is the Mute Swan, which has an orange bill

CANADA GOOSE
(BRANTA CANADENSIS)

The Canada Goose can be found right across North America at different times of year; it flies in a V formation during migrations and often stops to feed. Its diet consists of aquatic vegetation, grain, grass, and small aquatic animals, and populations are increasing as it extends its range into city parks and golf courses. Birds in the northern areas tend to be smaller and there is some color variation, with eastern birds generally paler. The Canada Goose makes a nest in a hollow lined with plant material and down, usually in an open area close to water. The 2–12 eggs are incubated by the female for 25–30 days. The male defends his mate and chicks aggressively, initially warning and then attacking if an intruder persists. Young birds are downy and leave the nest shortly after hatching though they remain with their parents until the following spring.

SIZE Length, 2–3½ ft; wingspan, 4–6 ft
DESCRIPTION Black head and neck, white "chin strap" and breast, dark back, white undertail coverts
HABITAT Ponds, marshes, grassland, open farmland
SIMILAR SPECIES Brant Goose is usually smaller with dark front and belly

MALLARD (ANAS PLATYRHYNCHOS)

SIZE Length, 2 ft
DESCRIPTION Male has green head, gray body, white collar, yellow bill; female sandy brown with orange, black-marked bill. Bright blue patch on upper side of wing, edged in white
HABITAT Freshwater shallows, tidal marshes
SIMILAR SPECIES Male distinctive; female can be distinguished from other species by the bill

The Mallard is common across most of North America; it is also the ancestor of most domestic ducks. Though it lives in the wild, it is probably most familiar around cities and in parks where it may be fed; female mallards are the ones that quack. It dabbles for food, going tail-up to forage for aquatic plants, insects, snails, and small fish. The nest is built in vegetation close to water; in a hollow lined with grass, stems, and down, and contains 5–14 eggs. These are incubated for just under a month by the female; the chicks, which leave the nest shortly after they hatch, can fly after about 8 weeks. Juvenile Mallards look rather like the female bird, but the bill is dark olive in color.

(ANAS ACUTA) NORTHERN PINTAIL

The Northern Pintail is found across most of North America at different times of year; it breeds in the north and migrates south to winter. Preferring open areas, it is more common in the west. It dabbles for food in shallow water, foraging for snails, crustaceans, and small fish on the bottom. It will also eat seeds and insects. Like other dabbling ducks it can launch itself into flight from the water without needing to run across the surface. The nest is a hollow made of plant material and lined with down, containing 6–12 eggs. The female incubates these for about 26 days and the chicks leave the nest shortly after hatching; they do not fly for another 7 weeks. Juvenile Northern Pintails resemble the female.

SIZE Length, 1½–2 ft

DESCRIPTION Male has white breast, thin white stripe up to brown head, gray body, long, dark tail feathers; female buff-brown, long tail; grayish bill. Both have metallic brown-green patch on upper wing

HABITAT Marshes, lakes, open ponds

SIMILAR SPECIES Male unmistakable, female larger than most others

COMMON MERGANSER
(MERGUS MERGANSER)

SIZE Length, 2 ft
DESCRIPTION Male mostly white, black back, green head; female gray with rusty-red head and white throat
HABITAT Woodland lakes and rivers, generally freshwater
SIMILAR SPECIES Male distinct; female Red-breasted Merganser similar to female but contrast between head and neck coloring is clearer

The Common Merganser is found across much of North America at different times of year, moving southwards in winter. It can form quite large flocks, favoring wooded rivers and lakes in the breeding season. A diving duck, it pursues its prey underwater, hunting small frogs, fish, aquatic invertebrates, and newts. Like other mergansers, the Common Merganser has a long, narrow bill with a hooked mandible and serrated edges; it is sometimes called the "Sawbill" by hunters. It nests in a cavity in a tree or log, or among rocks, and the nest is lined with a mass of down; there are 9–12 eggs. These are incubated by the female for about a month; the chicks, which leave the nest soon after hatching, start flying at 8–10 weeks of age.

TURKEY VULTURE
(CATHARTES AURA)

The Turkey Vulture is widespread and glides over open country during the day, barely flapping its wings, scanning for food which this large, carrion-feeder detects by the smell. Ideally it prefers its meat to be quite ripe, making it easier to detach from the bones; feeding can be messy. Many birds will converge to feed on a single carcass, and the Turkey Vulture often roosts in flocks. There is no nest and 1–3 eggs are laid on the ground, in a cave, hollow log, or old building; these are incubated by both adults for about 40 days. Approximately 11 weeks after hatching the young birds are ready to leave. A juvenile has a darker gray head and bill, and can easily be mistaken for a Black Vulture. In winter the more northerly populations move southwards, away from snow-covered areas.

SIZE Length, 2 ft; wingspan, 5–5½ ft

DESCRIPTION Large; black-gray body, gray edging to wings, bare red head, yellow feet. Glides with wings held in shallow V shape

HABITAT Open country, woodland, farms

SIMILAR SPECIES Black Vulture has gray head, shorter tail; resembles juvenile except for tail and flight pattern

BALD EAGLE
(HALIAEETUS LEUCOCEPHALUS)

The Bald Eagle has been the symbol of the US since 1782, and is seen across most of North America, especially close to water. Endangered as recently as the 1970s, it is beginning to recover due to conservation programs. It eats carrion or steals fish from the Osprey, though it is an accomplished hunter. Large numbers will gather where food is easy to find, particularly at spawning runs. Its eyrie is a large heap of sticks, usually in a tall tree by water, and may be as high as 150 ft. The nest is not abandoned but revisited and repaired each year until being brought down by either its own weight or winter weather. Both adults incubate the 1–3 eggs for up to 35 days; chicks leave the nest about 10 weeks after hatching. Juveniles may take 5 years to attain their full adult plumage, getting whiter with each molt; initially they are mostly dark brown.

SIZE Length, 3 ft; wingspan, 6½ ft
DESCRIPTION White on head, neck, and tail, brown-black body; bright yellow bill
HABITAT Rivers, lakes, coastal areas
SIMILAR SPECIES Adult unmistakable; juvenile resembles young Golden Eagle but has larger head, shorter tail, less defined patterning

GOLDEN EAGLE
(AQUILA CHRYSAETOS)

An essentially solitary bird of prey, the Golden Eagle may be seen in pairs, but seldom in groups. Widespread, it is more common in the west and prefers wilderness areas well away from people. It soars with its wings held flat or slightly uplifted. It feeds on small mammals, birds, snakes, and carrion, though it is able to take a larger animal. There are persistent rumors about it taking livestock, particularly lambs, but it rarely does. The eyrie is a mass of sticks on a cliff or high in a tree, and a pair may use different sites, alternating between them in different years. The 2 eggs are incubated for as long as 44 days by both birds; chicks leave the nest 10 weeks after hatching. Juveniles are dark brown with a white wing patch, and a white tail with a black band at the tip; after 4 years they have their full adult plumage.

SIZE Length, 2½–3 ft; wingspan, 6½ ft
DESCRIPTION Dark brown plumage on body, golden nape
HABITAT Mountains, plains, open country
SIMILAR SPECIES Adult unmistakable; juvenile like young Bald Eagle but has smaller head, longer tail, more defined markings

OSPREY (PANDION HALIAETUS)

SIZE Length, 2 ft; wingspan, 5 ft

DESCRIPTION Long, narrow wings; dark body above, white below, white head with dark eye stripe; dark patch on underside of wings

HABITAT Coastal areas, some freshwater habitats

SIMILAR SPECIES Unmistakable, though when flying could be confused with gulls

The Osprey is sometimes called the "Fish Hawk" and is reasonably common in coastal areas; it is sometimes seen along rivers and above lakes inland. It feeds almost exclusively on fish, catching them by soaring over the water and diving down rapidly, talons first. Ospreys were threatened by the heavy use of pesticides, but populations are beginning to recover since many bans were introduced. The bulky nest is built in a tall tree – or in any tall structure near water, even on specially constructed platforms – and is reused year after year. It contains 2–4 eggs, usually incubated by the female for about a month. Young Ospreys are white and downy, and leave the nest about 8 weeks after they hatch. Female Ospreys may have darker streaking on the neck and juveniles are somewhat similar, but with white scaling on the back.

(CIRCUS CYANEUS) NORTHERN HARRIER

Common and widespread across most of North America, the Northern Harrier spends summer in the north and migrates south for the winter. It is usually seen flying low, gliding with its wings in a shallow V shape, hunting for small rodents, birds, frogs, and reptiles over the wetlands and open fields it prefers. Black wing tips and a barred tail show in flight. During migration it may soar, and the courtship display is acrobatic. The nest is built on a platform of reeds and grass in the marshes – it was previously called the Marsh Hawk – and contains 4–6 eggs which the female Northern Harrier incubates for just over a month. Young birds remain in the nest for up to 5 weeks and are fed by the female though the male brings the food to the nest. Juvenile birds resemble the female, but have cinnamon-colored undersides.

SIZE Length, 1½–2 ft; wingspan, 3½ ft

DESCRIPTION Long wings and tail; male light gray above, white rump, white underside with reddish spots; female brown above, white rump, brown streaks below

HABITAT Wetlands, marshes, open fields

SIMILAR SPECIES Unmistakable

RED-TAILED HAWK (BUTEO JAMAICENSIS)

SIZE Length, 2 ft; wingspan, 4 ft
DESCRIPTION Broad wings, short tail, heavy bill; dark brown back with pale mottling; white underneath, belly band of red streaks; varies with range. Most adults have reddish tail above, whiter beneath
HABITAT Woods, plains, prairies
SIMILAR SPECIES Rough-legged Hawk has long white tail

The Red-tailed Hawk is one of the commonest North American hawks and can be seen soaring above open country, especially if there are nearby woods providing nesting cover. It may sit on a post or telegraph pole for hours before spotting something significant and taking off to catch its prey. It is popular in agricultural areas because it mainly eats rodents; northern birds move south in winter. The Red-tailed Hawk's nest is substantial, built up to 70 ft high in a tree or on a cliff. A small cup in the center is lined with green shoots and 1–4 eggs are laid. These are incubated for anything between 27 and 33 days and the chicks remain in the nest for another 5 weeks. Adult coloration varies according to range. Juveniles lack the distinctive red tails; theirs are gray-brown with dark bars.

(FALCO SPARVERIUS) AMERICAN KESTREL

The most common, as well as the smallest, falcon in North America, the American Kestrel is found in both cities and open country. Birds in more northern habitats move south in winter. It often uses posts, wires, or convenient trees as lookouts when hunting, suddenly plunging down to catch mice, insects, or even small birds during winter: it was formerly known as the Sparrow Hawk. It does not build a nest; the 3–6 eggs are laid in a tree hole, building crevice, or disused magpie nest. These are incubated for about 30 days by the female with some help from the male, and the chicks are able to leave the nest after another month.

SIZE Length, 10½ in; wingspan, 2 ft

DESCRIPTION Small, long tail, hooked bill; russet crown, back, tail, double black stripes on white face; male has blue-gray wings which female lacks; buff breast, paler to white underside with dark spots

HABITAT Open country, deserts, urban areas

SIMILAR SPECIES Coloration is distinctive

BLUE GROUSE (DENDRAGAPUS OBSCURUS)

SIZE Length, 20 in

DESCRIPTION Large with short bill, long tail; male blue-gray, orange-yellow comb above eye, dark tail with gray tip, neck sac inflated only in display; female mottled gray-brown overall

HABITAT Open mixed or coniferous woodland, brushy lowland, mountain slopes

SIMILAR SPECIES Female resembles female Spruce Grouse, but is larger

Found in open lowland woods in summer, where it prefers places near large clearings, the Blue Grouse moves to higher areas in winter. During winter it eats pine needles, feeding off seeds, insects, and berries the rest of the year. The spring display is quite impressive: the male stands high up, often in a tree, inflating his yellow or purple neck sac which is surrounded by white, and spreading his tail. He then flies down and struts with a fanned tail and wings dragging. The 6–10 eggs are laid in a sheltered scrape lined with pine needles and grass and are incubated by the female for about 26 days. The chicks remain with her for approximately 3 months. The juvenile Blue Grouse is similar to the female in appearance.

(CENTROCERCUS UROPHASIANUS) SAGE GROUSE

A large ground-dwelling bird, the Sage Grouse is found across sagebrush flats in the western US, but populations are declining as this habitat disappears. Though it will eat other plants, it mainly feeds on sagebrush leaves and buds. The spring courtship display is remarkable. Groups of males gather on a display ground, a "lek", with each one having a defined area. They then perform a dance to attract the females, bobbing and strutting with the tail widely fanned and chest inflated: this shows 2 yellow-green air sacs which the male Sage Grouse can inflate and deflate rapidly, producing a loud popping sound. Following this, one male may mate with several females. The 7–12 eggs are laid in a shallow earth depression under the sagebrush and are incubated for about 26 days. The chicks remain with the female for some time after they hatch.

SIZE Length, 2½ ft

DESCRIPTION Large, long pointed tail; gray-streaked above, black below; male has black throat and white breast which is inflated in display

HABITAT Sagebrush plains and foothills

SIMILAR SPECIES Sharp-tailed Grouse much smaller and without distinctive black belly

WILD TURKEY
(MELEAGRIS GALLOPAVO)

The ancestor of the domestic bird, the Wild Turkey was once plentiful but populations decreased due to both hunting and habitat destruction. It is making a comeback, being introduced into new areas. It forages on the forest floor for seeds, nuts, acorns, berries, and insects, and is a strong flyer, roosting in trees at night. In spring the male struts in his own small forest clearing, displaying to females with tail feathers spread out, head back, and wings dragging, making a gobbling mating call. Several females may respond, 10 or more, and after mating they all disperse. The 8–16 eggs are laid in a shallow depression in the woods which is lined with leaves and grass; they are incubated by the female for about 4 weeks. Chicks are fluffy and able to fly within a few weeks, but stay with the female until the following spring. Juvenile birds resemble the females.

SIZE Length, 3 ft (female); 4 ft (male)
DESCRIPTION Huge body, thin neck, small head; male has bronze iridescent plumage, wing tips barred in white, bare blue and red head, long dark breast tuft; female smaller and duller, sometimes without breast tuft
HABITAT Open pine–oak forest, oak woods
SIMILAR SPECIES None

AMERICAN COOT (FULICA AMERICANA)

SIZE Length, 15½ in
DESCRIPTION Stocky, big lobed feet; dark gray body, black head and neck, ivory-colored forehead shield with reddish upper edge; whitish bill with band near tip
HABITAT Freshwater and saltwater marshes, wetlands
SIMILAR SPECIES Common Moorhen has red face shield

The American Coot can be seen in large flocks, containing hundreds of birds. In urban areas it may become almost tame; living on golf courses and in parks. It bobs its head while swimming, diving to the bottom to find fish and mollusks, but also dabbles for insects and pondweed on the surface. Its large feet make it possible for it to walk on aquatic vegetation and are also a swimming aid. The nest, which may be used throughout the year for resting, is generally built on a platform of marsh vegetation and weeds next to open water. The 8–25 eggs are incubated for about 25 days by both adults. The chicks' frontal shield is blue and red, which appears to trigger an automatic feeding response in the parents. Within 7–8 weeks the paler juveniles are independent; they have adult plumage by winter.

(CHARADRIUS VOCIFERUS) KILLDEER

The Killdeer, a common open-country bird across most of North America, eats earthworms, snails, and insects, feeding in large flocks; its name is derived from its call. It winters in the south and moves northwards with the spring, living both inland and on coasts. It nests on open ground, with 4 eggs usually laid in a bare scrape, sometimes with a few grass stems used as a lining. Incubation is by both adults and takes about 26 days. If there is any threat or danger one adult will do a convincing imitation of a bird with a broken wing, drawing predators away. Killdeer chicks leave the nest shortly after they hatch and fly within a month. They have only one breast band at first, but the second develops with the juvenile plumage.

SIZE Length, 10½ in
DESCRIPTION Lanky, long tail, slender wings; gray-brown above, white underparts, two black breast bands; pale gray legs and feet, long, thin dark bill. Rump shows red-orange in flight
HABITAT Grassy fields, lake and river shores
SIMILAR SPECIES Breast bands make it distinctive

COMMON SNIPE
(GALLINAGO GALLINAGO)

SIZE Length, 10½ in

DESCRIPTION Stocky, long bill, short legs and wings; striped head, brown mottled back, barred flanks. Rapid zig-zag flight

HABITAT Marshes, damp fields, muddy pond edges

SIMILAR SPECIES Distinctive shape, bill, plumage, and flight pattern

The Common Snipe, previously known as Wilson's Snipe, is found across most of North America in boggy areas with enough vegetation to provide cover. Solitary and secretive, it is most likely to be seen in flight having been disturbed. It forages for food, probing deep into mud with its long bill in jerky movements, searching for crustaceans, insects, and other small animals. Summer is spent breeding in the more northerly areas and it moves further south in winter. It breeds in marshes and damp places; during the display flight it vibrates its tail feathers, making a hooting noise. The 4 eggs are laid in a grass-lined depression and are incubated by the female for up to 3 weeks. Young Common Snipe are independent in about 20 days.

GREAT BLACK-BACKED GULL
(LARUS MARINUS)

The Great Black-backed Gull is common along northern coasts and is also found some way inland; its range is expanding southwards. It eats fish as well as the eggs and young of other seabirds, and may be seen scavenging round garbage dumps; it will also eat carrion. Despite this, nesting colonies sometimes contain other seabirds. It constructs a cup of seaweed, grass, and mosses to hold the 2–3 eggs which are incubated by both adults. Though the chicks leave the nest soon after hatching, they are unable to fly for about 2 months. A young Great Black-backed Gull takes 4 years to reach its mature plumage. The first winter it is checkered gray-brown, with lighter underparts and a black bill. This gradually changes with successive molts until by the third winter it closely resembles an adult bird, though there is still some brown on the wings.

SIZE Length, 2½ ft; wingspan, 5 ft

DESCRIPTION Large, long wings; big yellow bill; large white head, black upper parts, white below, pink legs

HABITAT Coastal areas, some in Great Lakes

SIMILAR SPECIES Size distinctive but year-old juveniles resemble those of Herring Gull

ATLANTIC PUFFIN
(FRATERCULA ARCTICA)

The Atlantic Puffin dives for fish, "flying" gracefully through the sea; it also eats crustaceans and mollusks. It tends to stay in the north, coming as far south as Virginia in the winter, though it usually remains offshore. In summer it lands in order to breed, nesting in large colonies on offshore islands. The nest is sometimes in a rock crevice, but is more often at the end of a burrow in soft earth. A single egg is laid and the female incubates it for 5–6 weeks; the young bird is independent almost 2 months later. In winter the Atlantic Puffin has a gray face and the bill is both smaller and less bright – several bright color plates have been shed; they regrow the following spring. The juvenile resembles a winter adult, but has a browner face and a small brownish bill; it takes 5 years for it to develop an adult one.

SIZE Length, 12½ in
DESCRIPTION Rounded head, multicolored bill; black plumage above, white below, white face; in winter adult has gray face, duller bill
HABITAT Atlantic coast, offshore and islands
SIMILAR SPECIES Only puffin on Atlantic coast

BLACK TERN (CHLIDONIAS NIGER)

SIZE Length, 9½ in

DESCRIPTION Breeding adult's body and head mostly black, dark gray back, wings, and tail, white undertail coverts; short black bill, dark legs and feet

HABITAT Lake shores, freshwater marshes

SIMILAR SPECIES Size and plumage distinctive

Black Tern populations have declined in many places, perhaps due to loss of habitat. Only seen in summer, it winters in the Southern Hemisphere. It breeds in small confined colonies in freshwater marshes and on lakeshores, generally inland. A graceful bird, it can be seen hovering above the water then dipping downwards to catch small fish, crustaceans, and flying insects. The Black Tern nest is built of marsh vegetation and usually floats; it contains 2–3 eggs which are incubated by both parents for about 3 weeks. Following hatching the chicks remain in the nest for a further 2–3 weeks until they begin to fly. Juvenile birds, and winter adults, are dark gray above and white below, with a dark crown and ear patch, and a dark shoulder bar.

(COLUMBA LIVIA) ROCK DOVE

The Rock Dove is an introduced species, coming originally from the Mediterranean area of Europe. It was domesticated and used for both food and carrying messages. Multicolored birds developed over centuries and escaped birds were the ancestors of the feral flocks now present in most areas, except for the tundra. The Rock Dove feeds on seeds and grain but will also eat fruit and scraps of bread. It builds a somewhat insecure nest on a sheltered ledge of a building, bridge, cliff, or even in a tree, and lays 1–3 eggs. They are incubated by both birds for between 2–3 weeks, and the chicks stay in the nest for another 7 weeks after hatching. Nesting takes place throughout the year and the adults may raise several broods in a season.

SIZE Length, 1 ft
DESCRIPTION Small round head, short straight bill, variable colors
HABITAT Urban areas, rocky habitats
SIMILAR SPECIES Feral Rock Doves are variable; they can look like several wild species

GREATER ROADRUNNER
(GEOCOCCYX CALIFORNIANUS)

The Greater Roadrunner's curious behavior makes it famous. A member of the cuckoo family, it prefers to run along the ground on its strong feet though it can fly if it needs to. It sometimes flicks up its tail or raises its crest and may take up a variety of strange positions when resting on a rock or fence post. It runs in fast bursts, catching a wide range of food including scorpions, lizards, large insects, snakes, small birds and mammals, particularly rodents. It is commonest in the southwestern deserts and may dash towards cover at speeds of up to 15 mph if disturbed. The Greater Roadrunner's nest is small and tidy and built in mesquite, a large cactus or shrub; it contains 3–6 eggs. Incubation takes 3 weeks and the chicks hatch at intervals. They stay in the nest for 2–3 weeks after hatching and are fed by both adults.

SIZE Length, 2 ft
DESCRIPTION Large, long tail; brown with green sheen, streaked black and white above, buff below, brown streaks on breast; distinctive crest and heavy bill
HABITAT Scrubby desert, mesquite groves
SIMILAR SPECIES Unmistakable

BARN OWL (TYTO ALBA)

SIZE Length, 1½ ft
DESCRIPTION White heart-shaped face, dark eyes; face edged with tan, light tan back with fine pale gray streaks; underside white to cinnamon
HABITAT Old buildings, barns, cliffs, trees
SIMILAR SPECIES Snowy Owl normally whiter, with small head and yellow eyes

The Barn Owl population is in decline; although the bird is widespread across much of North America, it is quite rare. Nocturnal, it hunts for mice and rats over meadows, woodland, or suburbs, and roosts during daylight in dark corners of urban or rural buildings, or sometimes on cliffs or in trees. Seen at night, maybe caught in lights, it has a ghostly appearance, especially if seen from below; female Barn Owls are lighter than the males. It does not build a nest; the 5–11 eggs are laid on a bare surface in a cavity such as a corner in a barn, attic, or cave. The female incubates them, usually alone, for up to 5 weeks. The chicks are ready to leave after another 8 weeks, but are not fully independent for another month.

(BUBO VIRGINIANUS) GREAT HORNED OWL

The Great Horned Owl, the best known and most widespread North American owl, is a fierce predator with a sharp, hooked bill, powerful talons, and a large appetite. Its yellow eyes and wide-spaced ear tufts give it a rather cat-like appearance. It tackles quite large prey, such as geese, skunks, rabbits, squirrels, and snakes, and hunts mainly at night. It is sometimes seen in daylight, often being mobbed by smaller birds, and may be spotted perched high up at dusk. The male's hooting is often answered by a lower-pitched hoot from the female. It does not build a nest of its own, but reuses an abandoned heron, hawk, or crow nest in a rocky crevice, tree, or cliff. The 2–4 eggs are incubated by the female for around 7 weeks. Both adults feed the fluffy chicks, and they are ready to leave the nest about 10 weeks after hatching.

SIZE Length, 2–2½ ft

DESCRIPTION Bulky; wide-spaced ear tufts; mottled gray-brown above, white throat, fine dark gray horizontal barring beneath yellow eyes

HABITAT Forest, open desert, urban areas

SIMILAR SPECIES Long-eared Owl smaller and more slender, lacking white throat

COMMON NIGHTHAWK
(CHORDEILES MINOR)

SIZE Length, 9½ in

DESCRIPTION Slender, long wings; mottled black-brown above, paler beneath, dusky barring, white across wing; male has white throat and tail band; slightly forked tail

HABITAT Woodland, farmland, suburbs

SIMILAR SPECIES Lesser Nighthawk paler, wings more rounded

The Common Nighthawk glides and flies high above the ground, its rather erratic wingbeats interspersed with easier strokes, catching insects. The male makes display flights on warm summer evenings, diving steeply. Despite the name it is not a hawk. Common across much of its range, numbers are now declining. It winters in the subtropics, including parts of Mexico. No nest is built; the 2 eggs are laid directly on a flat roof or the ground. They are incubated by the female for 20 days or so and both parents feed the chicks until they are able to leave about 3 weeks later. Birds in the east tend to be browner in color while northern birds are grayer; both the female and the juvenile have a buff-colored throat and wing bar.

CHIMNEY SWIFT
(CHAETURA PELAGICA)

Often accurately described as looking like a "cigar with wings", the Chimney Swift is found in eastern North America in summer; it winters in South American rainforests. It does not perch, instead clinging to vertical surfaces while roosting at night. Always on the wing during daylight, it flies fast with rapid wingbeats or sails with the wings held stiff; the tail is difficult to see in flight. It catches insects on the wing and has a distinctive chippering call. In the past the Chimney Swift would nest in a tree hole, but now the nest – a half-cup of twigs stuck together with saliva – is constructed inside a barn or chimney. The 4–5 eggs are incubated for up to 3 weeks by both parents, and the young leave the nest about 4 weeks later.

SIZE Length, 5½ in
DESCRIPTION Small, stubby tail; long, narrow, slim body; long curved wings; sooty brown overall with lighter throat
HABITAT Urban areas, woodland
SIMILAR SPECIES None in range

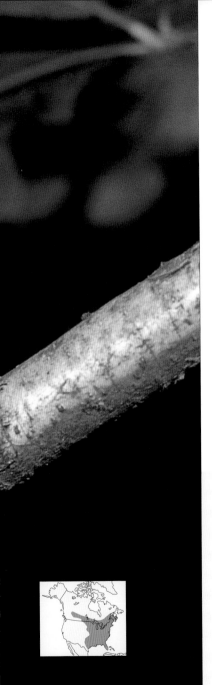

RUBY-THROATED HUMMINGBIRD
(ARCHILOCHUS COLUBRIS)

The only hummingbird encountered in the east, the tiny Ruby-throated Hummingbird migrates right across the Gulf of Mexico to winter in Central America. It will eat tiny flying insects and small spiders, though nectar from red tubular flowers is its preferred food. A solitary bird, it only joins another for mating. A nest of spider's web and plant down is built by the female, often near water, and 2 white eggs are incubated by her for 11–14 days. The young birds fledge after 2–4 weeks, and she will rear 2–3 similar clutches by herself. The male does defend the breeding area and its resources of nectar with some stylized displays, but the female also defends the nest during breeding and the nectar supply at other times. Juveniles are similar to the female in appearance, with a white throat and chin.

SIZE Length, 3¾ in
DESCRIPTION Small; long, straight, thin bill; bright green back, white underparts, male has black face and chin and iridescent throat
HABITAT Gardens, woodland edges
SIMILAR SPECIES Male's throat color distinctive, female similar to other female hummingbirds

BELTED KINGFISHER (CERYLE ALCYON)

SIZE Length, 1 ft

DESCRIPTION Shaggy crest, heavy bill; blue-gray above and on head, white collar, blue-gray breast band; male has white belly, female has rusty-red belly band across white

HABITAT Rivers, streams, ponds, lakes, estuaries

SIMILAR SPECIES Male unmistakable; female Ringed Kingfisher larger with all-rust belly, rusty underwing

Across most of North America the Belted is the only kingfisher. It is common and birds are often seen close to water in woodlands; the loud, rattling call may also be heard as it flies between its perches. It watches the water from one of these; when it spots a fish it hovers above it in the air and then dives down beak-first. It also eats frogs, tadpoles, and insects. A solitary bird, it defends its territory against incomers, only really encountering others during the breeding season. No nest is built, but a tunnel — which can be 7 ft long — is dug in the side of a steep riverbank. The 5–8 eggs are laid on bare soil at the end and are incubated for about 3–4 weeks. The young birds leave the burrow when they are fully fledged.

(PICOIDES VILLOSUS) HAIRY WOODPECKER

Widespread across North America, the Hairy Woodpecker is fairly common, inhabiting mature woodland with large trees. It drills into these to find wood-boring insects under the bark, though it also eats seeds and berries; it drums on the surface of trees to proclaim the existence of its territory. It excavates a hole in a dead tree branch high above the ground for use as a nest site, and often uses the same one for some years. Both adults share the incubation of the 4–7 eggs for about 2 weeks, the male looking after them at night and the female during the day. About 4–5 weeks after they hatch, the young birds can fend for themselves and are ready to leave the nest. Disused woodpecker holes are often used by other animals, as well as some other birds.

SIZE Length 9½ in

DESCRIPTION White back, black crown and forehead, black eye stripe, white face and underparts, wings black with white spots; male has red patch on nape; long, sturdy bill

HABITAT Dense and open forests

SIMILAR SPECIES Downy Woodpecker almost identical but smaller and bill shorter

BLUE JAY (CYANOCITTA CRISTATA)

SIZE Length, 11 in
DESCRIPTION Crested, broad wings; blue above, gray-white underneath with black necklace, black barring on wings and tail, white patches on tail, other tail feathers white
HABITAT Suburbs, parks, woodland
SIMILAR SPECIES Coloration distinctive, often mimics calls of other birds

The noisy, showy Blue Jay is found across most of eastern North America and is sometimes seen in the west and northwest. It is a regular visitor to birdfeeders, especially enjoying sunflower seeds. Some birds migrate southwards during fall in large flocks. The Blue Jay eats seeds, nuts, fruit, and insects. It has a harsh voice, like other jays, and often does excellent imitations of other birds, particularly the Red-shouldered Hawk. The nest is situated as high as 50 ft above the ground on a branch or in the crotch of a tree; it is bulky and made with twigs, moss, and leaves. The female incubates the 3–5 eggs for approximately 17 days, and the young Blue Jays leave the nest about 3 weeks after hatching.

(CORVUS BRACHYRHYNCHOS) AMERICAN CROW

Big and black, the American Crow is the largest of the crows. It is common across North America, ranging northwards during summer. Originally a woodland species, it has proved highly adaptable and now lives almost anywhere. It is also intelligent and resourceful, and has a system of communicating calls which warn members of the loose breeding colonies, perhaps hundreds of birds, of possible danger. This system is also used to indicate the presence of food. The American Crow is a predator and will eat most things, including other birds' chicks and eggs. The nest is well constructed from sticks and plant material, and located in a tree. The 3–6 eggs are incubated for approximately 17 days and young crows are ready to leave the nest and start living independently after about 5 weeks.

SIZE Length, 1½ ft
DESCRIPTION Large, powerful bill; short tail, broad wings; entirely black. Distinct cawing sound
HABITAT Open country, cities
SIMILAR SPECIES Fish Crow smaller, distinguished also by call

COMMON RAVEN (CORVUS CORAX)

SIZE Length, 2 ft
DESCRIPTION Large, long wings, heavy bill; all black with neck ruff; low, resonant voice
HABITAT Mountains, desert, forest, some suburbs
SIMILAR SPECIES Chihuahuan Raven is slightly smaller; different call, shorter bill

The Common Raven, already numerous in the north and west, is spreading into the east, even extending its range into some cities. It makes a wide variety of sounds, including whistles and screams. Markedly resourceful and intelligent, it easily learns to adapt its behavior to a new situation. It often feeds at garbage dumps and will also eat carrion, rodents, insects, and eggs and chicks of other birds. Pairs mate for life and are often seen as they soar together high in the sky. The nest, made from sticks and branches, is large and loose; it is lined with wool or animal fur and located high up, in a tree or on a cliff face. The female incubates the 4–7 eggs for up to 3 weeks, and young Common Ravens are ready to fend for themselves, and leave the nest, about 5 weeks after they hatch.

(TACHYCINETA BICOLOR) TREE SWALLOW

Both widespread and common in most of North America, the Tree Swallow winters in the southern states and Central America. It can actually be seen in a variety of habitats, especially in huge flocks prior to migrating, but is always close to water. Tree Swallows often perch in long rows on branches or wires, and eat spiders and insects caught on the wing. When other food is scarce, during winter, it will eat berries. A cup-shaped nest, lined with feathers, is built in an abandoned woodpecker hole, tree hollow, or nest box. There are 4–6 eggs, incubated by the female for about 2 weeks, and the young birds are able to leave the nest about 2–3 weeks later. Juveniles are gray-brown above and often have an indistinct dusky breast band.

Size Length, 5³/₄ in
Description Stocky; broad wings, shallow forked tail; metallic blue-black above, white below
Habitat Woodland near water
Similar species Violet-green Swallow has white on cheek and rump sides, variable iridescent color

AMERICAN ROBIN
(TURDUS MIGRATORIUS)

Often seen in suburban gardens, the American Robin is both common and widespread across North America, going right up into Canada and the far north in summer. It is also one of the best known American birds, its distinctive plumage making it easy to identify. It has a distinctive caroling song. It can be seen on lawns, its head cocked to one side, looking for earthworms; insects and berries also form an important part of the diet. The nest is built in a shrub, tree, or on a building; it is a sturdy cup of twigs, plant roots, and mud, lined with soft material. There are 3–4 eggs which are incubated by the female, and the young robins leave the nest 2–3 weeks after hatching. Female robins are slightly duller than males, and juvenile birds do not have the red breast; they are spotted instead.

SIZE Length, 10 in
DESCRIPTION Sturdy; long legs and tail; gray-brown above, white throat, orange-red breast, blackish head and tail, yellow bill
HABITAT Woodland, swamps, urban parks and gardens
SIMILAR SPECIES Unmistakable

EASTERN BLUEBIRD
(SIALIA SIALIS)

Once declining, the numbers of Eastern Bluebird are now improving; the main problem was competition for nest sites and specially designed nest boxes are being used to address this. In addition to nesting, the boxes may also be used to rest in during the day. It is found in small groups in open country and may frequently be seen perched on fence posts or wires. It eats insects, spiders, and berries, and also visits birdfeeders. It nests in a box, natural cavity or old woodpecker hole, building a loose cup shape on the bottom out of plant stems and grass. The female incubates the 2–7 eggs for around 2 weeks, and the young Eastern Bluebirds are independent about 3 weeks after they hatch. Juveniles are brownish and heavily spotted, though with a hint of blue above.

Size Length, 7 in
Description Stocky, short tail, stout bill, short wings; deep blue above, chestnut throat, sides of neck, breast, and flanks; white belly and underparts; female is duller
Habitat Open woodland, farmland, parks, forest edges
Similar species Western Bluebird has blue throat and different range

CEDAR WAXWING (BOMBYCILLA CEDRORUM)

SIZE Length, 7½ in

DESCRIPTION Round body, crested head; brown-gray above, yellow below, white undertail coverts, yellow and white wing markings, red spot on wing, yellow tail tip, black mask with white edge, black chin

HABITAT Trees with berries

SIMILAR SPECIES Bohemian Waxwing grayer with chestnut undertail, gray belly

The Cedar Waxwing is found across most of North America at various times of year and is almost always seen in large flocks, except during breeding. The flocks move around a lot in winter as they search for supplies of berries, which the Cedar Waxwing particularly likes, though it will also eat flower petals and flying insects. It builds a loose nest from twigs, grass, and berries, lined with moss, which is woven onto a horizontal branch of a tree in its breeding area. This can be as high as 50 ft above the ground. The 3–6 eggs are incubated for about 2 weeks and the young birds are ready to feed independently and look after themselves about 17–19 days later. Juveniles have similar coloring to the adults but are streaked beneath.

(DENDROICA PETECHIA) YELLOW WARBLER

The Yellow Warbler is widespread and common across much of North America; it winters in the tropics, and some birds go to Mexico. It often prefers woodland along streams, and forages for food among the foliage, usually at mid-level, eating spiders and insects. It also nests in the trees or shrubs, building a small cup of plant material in the crotch of a branch. The nest is lined with down and is sometimes used by the Cowbird before the Yellow Warbler can lay its own eggs. In these circumstances, the Yellow Warbler will simply build another floor over the interloper's egg and start again; some nests have been found with several floors. The 4–5 Yellow Warbler eggs are incubated by the female for 9–10 days, and the young birds leave about 10–12 days later. Juvenile birds look like the females.

SIZE Length, 5 in

DESCRIPTION Short tail, thick bill; yellow overall, dark eye; wings and tail yellow-olive with yellow markings; male has chestnut stripes on breast and flanks; female duller, may have faint streaks

HABITAT Wet open woodland, willows, alders

SIMILAR SPECIES Male Wilson's Warbler has black cap; female very alike

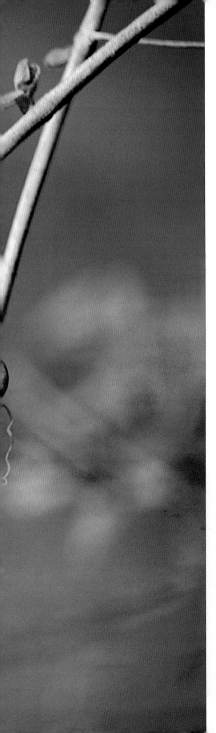

SCARLET TANAGER

(PIRANGA OLIVACEA)

The male Scarlet Tanager is most striking in summer, when it lives in leafy northeastern forests; when it migrates southwards for the winter, the male's plumage is much more like that of the less conspicuous female. It usually forages for food high in the tree canopy, though it sometimes comes lower down while migrating. It eats insects, caterpillars, and spiders as well as berries, and its considerable appetite for pests has made it popular with gardeners. It nests in a tree as high as 75 ft above the ground, and the nest is built at the tip of a horizontal branch. It is a shallow cup of leaves and grasses and holds 3–5 eggs. The female incubates them for about 2 weeks, and the young birds are able to leave the nest after around 10–12 days.

SIZE Length, 7 in

DESCRIPTION Thick gray bill; male has black wings and tail, white wing linings; brilliant red in breeding season, greenish-yellow in winter; female greenish-yellow with darker wings and tail, white wing linings

HABITAT Leafy forest

SIMILAR SPECIES Male distinctive; female similar to female Summer Tanager, but tail green beneath instead of grayish

SONG SPARROW (MELOSPIZA MELODIA)

SIZE Length, 5½–7½ in

DESCRIPTION Stocky, round head, long tail, stout bill, pinkish legs; variable coloring, generally streaky red-brown above, heavily striped beneath, central breast spot, white belly, light gray central crown stripe

HABITAT Dense thickets by rivers, parks, back yards

SIMILAR SPECIES Savannah Sparrow lacks breast spot

The Song Sparrow often hides in dense cover, though it also inhabits parks and suburban gardens where it can become quite tame. It is the most widespread sparrow in North America and is rarely seen in flocks, generally living in pairs or family groups. It eats seeds, grain, berries, and insects, and will come to birdfeeders in some places. The Song Sparrow nest is a cup of stems and grass built on or near the ground, though in a place where it is always well obscured by vegetation. It lays 3–6 eggs which are incubated by the female for about 2 weeks, and the young birds are independent after approximately 10 days. The pair of adults will often raise several broods each season.

(PASSERINA CYANEA) INDIGO BUNTING

The Indigo Bunting is rarely seen in the west; part of its range, however, overlaps with that of the western Lazuli Bunting and there is some interbreeding. It migrates southwards in winter, to Mexico, the West Indies, and Central America; some go to southern Florida. In the east the Indigo Bunting is common in woodlands and farmlands in summer. It can be seen foraging on the ground in flocks, hunting for insects and seeds; it also eats berries in fall. It nests in trees or bushes, up to 15 ft from the ground, weaving a tidy cup from strips of bark, grass, and leaves. There are 3–5 eggs which the female bird incubates for around 11–14 days. Young Indigo Buntings are ready to leave the nest about 10 days after they hatch.

SIZE Length, 5½ in

DESCRIPTION Short tail, stout bill; breeding male indigo blue overall; female and fall male brown, fine streaks on chest, blue tint to tail

HABITAT Woodland clearings, farmland, brushy pasture

SIMILAR SPECIES Male Blue Grosbeak larger with bigger bill, wide cinnamon wing bars

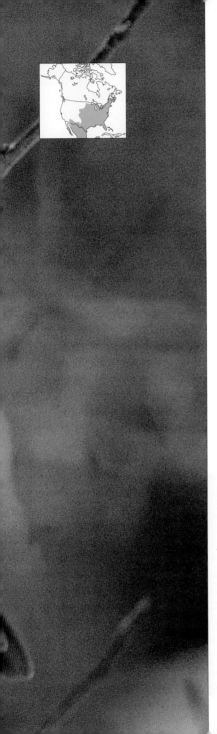

NORTHERN CARDINAL
(CARDINALIS CARDINALIS)

Common and with its range expanding, the Northern Cardinal lives in a variety of habitats, even city parks and back yards, as long as there is enough cover. It generally feeds on the ground and out in the open, eating fruit, seeds, and insects. It is a frequent visitor to birdfeeders during winter and is especially fond of sunflower seeds – the increasing availability of food from feeders may be one of the reasons behind the extension of its range. It pairs for life and pairs return to the same breeding area. The nest is constructed in a tree or shrub, up to 12 ft from the ground, and is rather loosely woven from twigs and plant material. It contains 3–4 eggs, incubated by the female for just under 2 weeks. The male provides food and helps feed the young after hatching. The juvenile is reddish-buff and has a black bill.

Size Length, 8¾ in
Description Crest, long tail, large triangular bill; male bright red with black face and throat and red bill; female olive-buff with reddish crest, wings and tail
Habitat Forests, swamps, thickets, parks, suburban back yards
Similar species Coloration distinctive

RED-WINGED BLACKBIRD
(AGELAIUS PHOENICEUS)

Found right across North America on all sorts of wet ground, the Red-winged Blackbird is both widespread and common. More northerly populations move southwards in winter. It forms large flocks, often with other blackbirds, except during the breeding season, and is sometimes considered a pest due to the volume of grain these eat in spring. It does, however, also catch large quantities of insect pests during the nesting season which would otherwise cause serious damage to crops. It also eats spiders and seeds. The nest is built close to the ground and is a sturdy grass cup attached to reeds or in a large bush. The Red-winged Blackbird lays 3–5 eggs which the female incubates for about 10–12 days. The young birds are capable of looking after themselves 2 weeks after hatching; the juvenile looks like the female.

SIZE Length, 8¾ in
DESCRIPTION Fairly short tail, rounded wings; male black with bright red and buff-yellow shoulder patch; female streaked brown, buff eyebrow.
HABITAT Freshwater marshes, farmland, open fields
SIMILAR SPECIES Male Tricolored Blackbird has dark red and white wing patch

EVENING GROSBEAK
(COCCOTHRAUSTES VESPERTINUS)

Size Length, 8 in

Description Short tail, short, pointed wings, massive bill; male has dark olive-brown head, neck, and breast, bright yellow forehead and eyebrow, yellow body, black wings and tail, large white wing patch; female grayish-gold, black wings, white-marked tail

Habitat Mixed woodlands, back yards

Similar species Goldfinch smaller, with much smaller bill

Both the range and numbers of the Evening Grosbeak vary from year to year, sometimes considerably. It is often seen in large flocks high in the trees. It eats seeds, berries, fruit, and buds, and will also eat insects; flocks can be attracted to garden feeders to feast on any sunflower seeds available. The nest is built in woodland, near the tip of a tree branch in dense cover. It is an insecure-looking construction, a bowl of small twigs and roots, and there may be several Evening Grosbeak nests fairly close to one another. The female incubates the 3–4 eggs for up to 2 weeks, and the young birds can fend for themselves after another 2 weeks. The juvenile bird looks like the female.

RED CROSSBILL
(LOXIA CURVIROSTRA)

The Red Crossbill lives in conifer forests but flocks search around for pine cones, the main part of the diet; they may move completely if the cone crop fails. It eats insects as well as pine nuts, and the specialist bill has developed to enable it to open the pine cone easily and remove the seeds. It breeds at any time of year, even in the deepest winter, as long as food is abundant. The nest is built in a conifer well above the ground; it is a tidy but shallow cup of twigs, roots, and moss, lined with lichens and fur. The female Red Crossbill incubates the 3–5 eggs for about 2 weeks and the young birds are independent and able to leave the nest around 15–17 days after they hatch. The juvenile is tinted with orange and has dusky streaks.

SIZE Length, 6¼ in

DESCRIPTION Stocky; short tail, large bill with crossed tip; male mottled brick-red, dark wings and tail; female mottled olive-gray, darker wings, dull yellow underparts and rump

HABITAT Coniferous woods

SIMILAR SPECIES White-winged Crossbill has two broad white wing bars

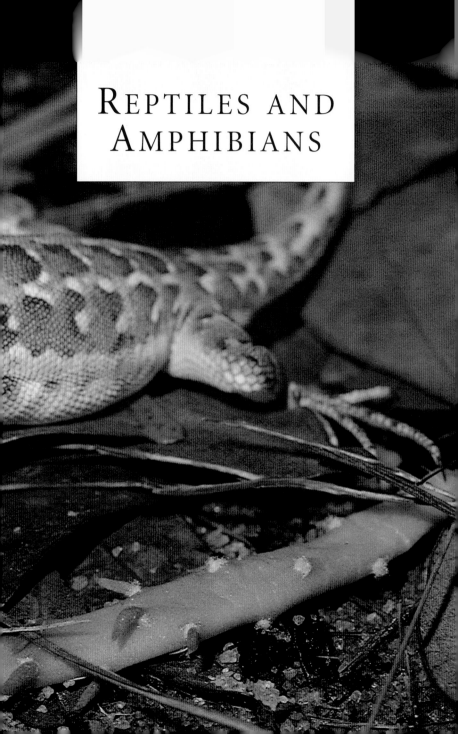

REPTILES AND AMPHIBIANS

COMMON SNAPPING TURTLE
(CHELYDRA SERPENTINA)

SIZE Length, 8–18 in; weight, 10–45 lb

DESCRIPTION Powerful jaws, long, saw-toothed tail; black to brown carapace with 3 distinct keels

HABITAT Varied; freshwater

SIMILAR SPECIES Alligator Snapping Turtle larger, lacks prominent tail ridges

A fairly large turtle, the Common Snapping is a formidable predator, eating fish, invertebrates, birds, reptiles, small mammals, and carrion, but also aquatic vegetation. It is generally found in slow-moving or still lakes with plenty of vegetation. As it can travel some distance overland to reach a new body of water or nesting site it is quite likely to be encountered out of the water, when it may be particularly aggressive. It does spend most of its time in the water, often buried in mud, and can lure fish with a pink, worm-like growth on its tongue. It mates from spring to fall but fertilization can be delayed, sometimes for years. Up to 50 eggs are laid and are incubated for 2–4 months.

PAINTED TURTLE
(CHRYSEMYS PICTA)

The Painted Turtle is the most widespread turtle in North America and one of the commonest. The stripes on the head are yellow, changing to red on the neck; these do not vary greatly in width. The legs have red stripes. It spends much of its time resting out of the water, basking on logs, branches, or other suitable perches. A sociable turtle, large numbers may be seen during early mornings and afternoons in spring basking together, even piling on top of each other if there is not enough space. It is likely to re-enter the water if disturbed. Basking raises the Painted Turtle's body temperature and activates digestive enzymes. It is generally omnivorous, eating a variety of invertebrates and vegetation, but becomes more exclusively herbivorous as it grows older.

SIZE Length, 4–7 in

DESCRIPTION Green to black unkeeled carapace, brightly marked with yellow and red; yellow and red stripes on head and legs, head often with yellow spots

HABITAT Still or slow-moving water with vegetation and basking places

SIMILAR SPECIES Smaller than Redbelly Turtle

SPINY SOFTSHELL
(TRIONYX SPINIFERUS/APALONE SPINIFERA)

SIZE Length, 5–10 in
DESCRIPTION Olive-green to brown; females are larger with spiny projections on leading edge of shell
HABITAT Mostly fast-flowing rivers, also marshy areas, still water
SIMILAR SPECIES Smooth Softshell lacks projections on shell

The Spiny Softshell's shell is flat and somewhat disc-shaped with a leathery covering rather than the hard, bony plates of most other turtles. Though only the female develops the spiny projections at the front, the male's shell may have a rough texture, with lots of small projections and bumps all over the surface. Primarily living in rivers, it is a powerful swimmer and highly aquatic; it feeds mainly on invertebrates and crustaceans but is quick enough to catch small fish and crayfish. It can also move quickly on land, but will return to the water with equal speed if disturbed. Most of its time is spent partially buried in sand or mud on the river bed, occasionally extending its long neck and snorkel-like nose to the surface in order to breathe.

DESERT TORTOISE
(GOPHERUS AGASSIZII)

The Desert Tortoise's burrow is a valuable stable-temperature refuge in its desert habitat, and its forelegs are long and broad, well-adapted for digging. The burrow may be up to 30 ft long and the eggs are laid 1–10 inches below the surface. A herbivore, it feeds on a variety of plants, including cacti, flowers, any green vegetation, and fruit; it obtains most of the water it needs through this diet. It usually feeds in the morning when it is cooler. There are separate feeding and habitation areas, and there is little sign of territorial behavior, though Desert Tortoises will sometimes ram each other on meeting. Now a protected species, it was very popular as a pet and the population is recovering only slowly, largely because adult females do not breed until they are nearly 20 years old. Loss of habitat has also been a factor in their decline.

SIZE Length, 9–14½ in
DESCRIPTION High-domed brown carapace with deep concentric lines, lighter in center when young
HABITAT Sandy desert, scrubland
SIMILAR SPECIES Gopher Tortoise very similar; head a darker grayish-black

LEATHERBACK
(DERMOCHELYS CORIACEA)

An endangered animal and the world's largest turtle, the Leatherback has a unique blue-black leathery carapace with pronounced ridges. It may be found quite close to the shore but is a powerful swimmer and primarily an open ocean species, traveling immense distances and feeding mainly on jellyfish. It can regulate its body temperature better than other turtles and occurs along the length of the Atlantic coast and up the Pacific, sometimes being found as far north as Alaska. Nesting, however, takes place much further south and there are nesting sites around the Gulf of Mexico and Florida. At night, any time from spring to fall but especially in summer, the female comes ashore to lay her eggs. She may lay almost 200 at one time and comes back over a period of some weeks, laying several similar clutches.

SIZE Length, 4–7 ft; weight, 650–1000+ lb
DESCRIPTION Enormous; leathery with no scales but with several keels; dark color
HABITAT Pelagic but found around coastlines
SIMILAR SPECIES None

LOGGERHEAD
(CARETTA CARETTA)

The Loggerhead is the most common sea turtle found along the coast of North America, even though it is endangered and not especially widespread. It is omnivorous and eats various marine invertebrates and plants. On summer nights, generally in warm water around the Gulf but occasionally further north, the female Loggerhead comes ashore to lay her eggs. The male also comes nearer inshore and they mate shortly after – or just before – the eggs are deposited in the sand. Though the female might lay as many as 100 eggs before she returns to the sea, many hatchlings will not live to adulthood. Some are drawn toward highways instead of the sea, confused by lights, and get run over; many Loggerheads, adults included, are caught and consequently drown in fishing nets.

SIZE Length, 3–4 ft; weight, 180–400 lb
DESCRIPTION Brown heart-shaped carapace
HABITAT Open seas, bays
SIMILAR SPECIES Hawksbill has overlapping scales; Green Turtle has 1 rather than 2 pairs of scales between the eyes

DESERT IGUANA
(DIPSOSAURUS DORSALIS)

The Desert Iguana is generally
herbivorous, unlike most iguanids, feeding
on creosote bushes and other vegetation.
It will also eat carrion and small
invertebrates. During the heat of the day it
is active, basking and even feeding in the
highest temperatures. If the ground
becomes too hot it climbs up into a bush
or withdraws to shelter in the rocks or an
old, enlarged rodent burrow. The burrows
are also useful when it is threatened by its
predators, such as birds of prey or large
snakes, and are used at night and during
hibernation. The burrow entrance will
often be blocked while it is occupied,
perhaps to regulate the temperature
within. The Desert Iguana is usually active
from spring through mid or late summer,
and mates soon after awakening in the
spring; as many as 8 eggs are produced
shortly after. The young iguanas are 3–4
inches long when they hatch.

SIZE Length including tail, 10–16 in
DESCRIPTION Large, stocky, low crest along back; dark
  head, lighter body and tail, often spotted with
  gray or white
HABITAT Sandy scrub, creosote flats, rocky foothills in
  desert
SIMILAR SPECIES Chuckwalla has no dorsal crest

EASTERN FENCE LIZARD
(SCELOPORUS UNDULATUS)

SIZE Length including tail,
3½–7½ in

DESCRIPTION Rough, raised scales;
gray to brown, dark wavy
crossbars, chevrons, or back
stripes; males with bluish
patches on belly sides and 2
blue patches on throat

HABITAT Dry woodlands, prairies,
brush, farmlands

SIMILAR SPECIES Sagebrush Lizard
rusty behind front legs, black
bar on shoulder

North America's most widely distributed lizard, the
Eastern Fence Lizard is one of the spiny lizards, so
called because of the pointed scales (rather than
spines) on the back. Both color and markings are
very variable, perhaps unsurprisingly given its
range. An insectivore, it feeds on beetles and other
small invertebrates during the day, and it also
spends time basking in the hot sun. In prairies and
grassland areas it usually lives on the ground, but in
more wooded environments it tends to be arboreal;
it is a good climber and is frequently seen on trees,
log piles, or fences. After hibernating during the
winter, it mates in spring. Younger females may only
lay a single clutch of eggs in a season, but an older
female may well produce up to 4 separate ones. The
hatchlings appear in late summer or early fall.

TEXAS HORNED LIZARD
(PHRYNOSOMA CORNUTUM)

The best known horned lizard in North America, the Texas Horned Lizard is probably the most striking with its two long head spines. These, doubtless, function as a deterrent to predators, but it generally relies on camouflage while in the open. If it is threatened, it usually attempts to hide in a burrow or among rocks and vegetation, though it will sometimes adopt a more assertive approach, hissing, advancing on the attacker, and squirting blood from the corners of its eyes. Despite all of this it is preyed upon by larger lizards, snakes, birds of prey, and coyotes. It can easily withstand high temperatures and is active during the day, hunting small insects, especially ants. It breeds in summer and large clutches of eggs – sometimes 30 or more – are laid in a burrow.

SIZE Length including tail, 2½–6 in

DESCRIPTION Small, flattish, characteristic spines and horns, short tail; mottled, brown-red or orange

HABITAT Arid, with sparse vegetation

SIMILAR SPECIES The two enlarged back head spines distinguish it from others

GILA MONSTER
(HELODERMA SUSPECTUM)

The largest lizard and the only venomous one found in North America, the Gila Monster is also easily recognized due to its striking coloration and short, thick tail. It has powerful jaws and sharp-edged, grooved teeth that deliver venom secreted from glands in the mouth as the lizard bites down on its victim. Though Gila Monster bites are very painful to humans, they are rarely fatal. The venom is used defensively, but also as a way of subduing prey. It feeds on reptiles, small mammals, ground-nesting birds and their eggs, and spends a lot of time under the ground. Though it can be active during the day, it usually hunts at night. The Gila Monster uses abandoned burrows, but will also dig its own; it is a powerful digger, and also a good climber.

SIZE Length including tail, 1½–2 ft
DESCRIPTION Large, stocky, short tail; bright red, orange, pink, or yellow alternating with black stripes; black forked tongue
HABITAT Scrub, desert, juniper-oak woodland
SIMILAR SPECIES None

COMMON/NORTHERN
WATER SNAKE (NERODIA SIPEDON)

SIZE Length, 2–4½ ft
DESCRIPTION large, usually dark; darker bands on neck becoming alternating blotches on back and sides
HABITAT Freshwater wetlands
SIMILAR SPECIES Southern Water Snake has dark marking between eyes and mouth; Cottonmouth larger, swims with head above water

With a superficial similarity to the Cottonmouth, the Common Water Snake is often persecuted and may be killed on sight. It is not venomous, however, although it will bite if under threat. It prefers slow-flowing or still water though it can be found in any freshwater habitat, and may be seen basking on a rock, branch, or tree stump during the day. It will dive into the water if disturbed and is a strong swimmer. It feeds on frogs and other amphibians, invertebrates, reptiles, the occasional small mammal, and fish; the belief that it significantly depletes fish stocks is unfounded. It mates in spring or summer and may have over 100 young, though the average is probably much less. Perhaps unsurprisingly, pregnant females are normally heavily distended. The young, born in late summer or fall, have vivid patterning; adults darken with age.

RINGNECK SNAKE

(DIADOPHIS PUNCTATUS)

The harmless Ringneck Snake is secretive, hiding beneath leaf litter, inside hollow logs, or under flat rocks; large numbers may congregate in a single hiding place. It is mostly nocturnal and infrequently seen in the open. If disturbed it may hide its head and curl its tail upside down, exposing the bright underside. Should this not be enough to deter an attacker it will discharge a foul-smelling musk and thrash about when picked up. Though not aquatic, it prefers habitats close to water; it eats a lot of amphibians as well as invertebrates and small reptiles. A clutch of up to 10 eggs is produced in summer and the nest is frequently communal. There are 12 subspecies, all varying slightly in pattern and color, but otherwise much alike.

SIZE Length, 1–2½ ft
DESCRIPTION Smooth scales; gray or olive above; yellow, orange, or red collar and underside; belly often spotted
HABITAT Woodland, prairies, scrub; often close to water
SIMILAR SPECIES Brown Snake juveniles have yellow collar, scales keeled rather than smooth

MILK SNAKE
(LAMPROPELTIS TRIANGULUM)

The Milk Snake is widespread, with a range from Canada down to Ecuador, and is also common. It is secretive and rarely seen during the day when it seeks shelter among logs, rocks, or in farm buildings. It was once erroneously believed to suckle milk from cows – hence the name – but it actually eats rodents, especially mice, birds, and reptiles including venomous snakes. It kills by means of constriction and is not venomous itself. It seizes its victim behind the head, wrapping coils around it until it suffocates. Typically, it swallows food head first, stretching its loosely jointed jaws to do so. It mates in spring and the clutch of about 10 eggs is laid in summer, often under logs. About 8 weeks later the young snakes hatch; they are 5–10 inches long.

SIZE Length, 2–3 ft

DESCRIPTION Smooth scales; color varies from gray with brown, black-edged blotches to "coral snake mimics" with colored bands; some with V- or Y-shaped marking on neck

HABITAT Varies; dry and damp conditions, woodlands to suburbs

SIMILAR SPECIES Some resemble Eastern Coral Snake, but red bordered with black, not yellow

BULLSNAKE (PITUOPHIS MELANOLEUCUS)

SIZE Length, 4–8 ft
DESCRIPTION Large, relatively small head; light colored, dark blotches on back and sides
HABITAT Mainly grasslands; brush, open pine woods
SIMILAR SPECIES Threat display may lead to confusion with rattlesnakes

The large and impressive Bullsnake is known in some areas of its range as the Pine Snake or Gopher Snake. It is a heavy constrictor and can put on an impressive display if encountered. It vibrates its tail, swells up, hisses loudly, and is very likely to bite. Usually active during the day, it also becomes increasingly active at night during the summer, and is often found hunting among vegetation or animal burrows. Though it will sometimes eat birds and eggs it mainly feeds on rodents which can be pests – mice, rats, pocket gophers – and is popular with farmers for this reason. The Bullsnake often uses a tortoise or mammal burrow as a refuge and will often hibernate with other species, including Rat Snakes and rattlesnakes.

(ELAPHE GUTTATA) CORN SNAKE

The Corn Snake is one of the rat snakes and, as that name suggests, rodents form an important part of its diet, making it popular with farmers. It is often seen around derelict farm buildings or any other places with lots of mice. A constrictor, it also eats birds, bats, amphibians, and reptiles. The day is spent in animal burrows or holes in stumps, and it emerges in the evening to hunt along the ground or in small-mammal burrows. Though it is usually found on the ground, it is an excellent climber – aided by its keeled scales – and will climb up into trees and bushes when chasing its prey. It is not dangerous but will usually vibrate its tail, coil, and rear up in a defensive display of aggressiveness if surprised.

SIZE Length, 2–6 ft

DESCRIPTION Slender, scales slightly keeled; often orange, also gray or brown, large back blotches alternate with smaller side ones; some have checkered underside and arrow mark on head

HABITAT Varies; woodlands, farmlands, rocky hills

SIMILAR SPECIES Kingsnakes and Milk Snakes may have similar marking but smooth scales

EASTERN CORAL SNAKE
(MICRURUS FULVIUS)

The bite of the Eastern Coral Snake can be fatal to humans; it should never, therefore, be handled. It is not normally aggressive, and both its mouth and teeth are small, but it can administer a powerful neurotoxin with the fixed fangs at the front of its upper jaw. The toxin is primarily designed to kill cold-blooded prey, and affects the respiratory and nervous systems. The Eastern Coral Snake is active during the day, often in the morning, hunting mainly for small lizards and snakes under leaf litter. It usually seeks cover when resting, once again using the leaf litter or sometimes logs. The eggs, which are laid in summer, hatch in the fall. The coral snakes are the only venomous North American snakes that produce eggs; the others, members of the viper family, bear live young.

Size Length, 2–4 ft
Description Black snout, distinctive red and black bands separated by yellow
Habitat Pine woods, rocky hills, woodland; dense vegetation
Similar species Scarlet Snake and similarly colored Milk Snake have red snouts and red bands divided by yellow not black

COTTONMOUTH
(AGKISTRODON PISCIVORUS)

The Cottonmouth, sometimes known as the Water Moccasin, is frequently aggressive; it is dangerous and its venom may be fatal to humans. Nights are usually spent hunting – it feeds mainly on fish and amphibians, but also eats small aquatic reptiles, birds, and mammals – and it may be seen basking in daylight. It is easily identified when swimming, as it is the only aquatic snake to swim with its head out of the water. Other aquatic species normally slither back into the water if disturbed, but the Cottonmouth will stand its ground. If especially agitated it will vibrate its tail then open its mouth in a wide gape, exposing the white lining. The temperature-sensitive receptors in the mouth allow the snake to detect, and strike out at, warm-blooded prey. The live young are venomous from birth.

SIZE Length, 2–6 ft
DESCRIPTION Heavy body, flat, lance-shaped head, keeled scales; dark body, patternless or with dark crossbands; mouth lining white
HABITAT Swamps, marshes, rivers, lakes, especially in wooded areas
SIMILAR SPECIES Other water snakes generally smaller

EASTERN DIAMONDBACK RATTLESNAKE

(CROTALUS ADAMANTEUS)

The most dangerous snake in North America, the Eastern Diamondback Rattlesnake is one of the most deadly snakes worldwide. It does not, generally, retreat from a threat but gives a warning by vibrating its rattle, the loosely interlocking terminal segments of its tail. It often shares the Gopher Tortoise's burrow in the winter, though it will also use a stump hole or brush pile. It is able to swim and is also found on the Florida Keys. It ambushes its prey, lying in wait under cover of vegetation and striking any animals that come close enough. These often include squirrels, cotton rats and other large rodents, rabbits, and birds; the Eastern Diamondback can help keep numbers of rodent pests down. The female produces young every other year and may give birth to as many as 20 in late summer or fall; however, numbers are declining as a result of both hunting and habitat destruction.

SIZE Length, 3–8 ft
DESCRIPTION Powerfully built; large head with 2 diagonal lines on sides, back has large dark diamond shapes edged with lighter scales
HABITAT Dry places; pine flatwoods, abandoned farms
SIMILAR SPECIES Other rattlesnakes generally smaller

AMERICAN ALLIGATOR
(ALLIGATOR MISSISSIPPIENSIS)

The largest reptile found in North America, the American Alligator has a huge, powerfully muscular body. It is now protected but earlier hunting, primarily for the skin, has led to a considerable reduction in numbers, as has continuing human encroachment on its habitat. It is a formidable predator, hunting fish, turtles, birds, mammals, and amphibians. It is also beneficial to animals in its environment, however; during droughts the water-filled "gator holes" it digs help to sustain other wildlife. Approximately 40 eggs are laid in summer in a nest made in a mound of rotting vegetation and are incubated there for about 2 months. The female is highly maternal for a reptile, guarding the eggs until they hatch, then opening the nest and carrying the young alligators to the water in her mouth. The young may remain with her for a year or more.

SIZE Length including tail, 6–18 ft
DESCRIPTION Enormous, armored, lizard-like, snout broad and rounded; black or gray, sometimes with lighter markings
HABITAT Freshwater; swamps, marshes, lakes, rivers
SIMILAR SPECIES American Crocodile has long, slender snout

GREEN FROG
(RANA CLAMITANS)

Found in a variety of habitats and with a large range, the Green Frog is very common. Its color varies considerably; northward into Canada it is darker, and in southern parts it is much more likely to be bronze — in fact it is usually known there as the Bronze Frog. Blue individuals have even been found. Plentiful in marshland, the Green Frog may move from it into neighboring meadows or damp woodlands when searching for the invertebrates on which it feeds. It breeds in spring or summer, and the males become territorial and highly vocal, issuing warning calls to intruders. The female Green Frog lays her spawn amid aquatic vegetation, as do most frogs.

SIZE Length, 2–4 in
DESCRIPTION Ridges along sides, prominent eardrums; green, brown, or bronze
HABITAT Shallow ponds and streams
SIMILAR SPECIES Similar to Milk Frog but has bands on hind legs

NORTHERN LEOPARD FROG
(RANA PIPIENS)

SIZE Length, 2–5 in

DESCRIPTION Medium sized; brown or green with 2 or 3 rows of brown spots, belly white

HABITAT Marshes, damp meadows, ponds, lakes, rivers

SIMILAR SPECIES Other leopard frogs are almost identical but male vocal sacs are invisible unless it is calling

The Northern Leopard Frog is a wanderer, and may travel as far as a mile from water, especially between hibernation and breeding. It leaves where it has been hibernating, a larger body of water such as a lake, and journeys to a smaller pool or breeding pond. Following breeding it then sets off through wet fields in search of a suitable deeper pond or lake where it will spend the winter. The mass of eggs produced is frequently fastened to vegetation in the breeding pond, but may also be laid directly on the bottom of the pool if conditions are right. The Northern Leopard Frog is the species often used in laboratories.

WOOD FROG
(RANA SYLVATICA)

Found further north than any other
amphibian, even living on the tundra
inside the Arctic Circle, the diurnal Wood
Frog may begin reproductive activities
even before the ice is completely gone
from the ponds. It hibernates in forests
through the winter, and enters the icy
water in order to breed; the ponds it
prefers are often quite shallow. It only
stays a few days, however, unlike most
species of frogs which inhabit their
breeding ponds for many weeks. The
Wood Frogs then disperse, and during
summer some may be found quite far
from water.

SIZE Length, 1¼–2¼ in
DESCRIPTION Dark to light brown or reddish,
  dark markings behind eyes; often light
  dorsal stripe
HABITAT Woodlands, grasslands, tundra
SIMILAR SPECIES Northern Chorus Frog has 3
  bold stripes on back

BULLFROG (RANA CATESBEIANA)

SIZE Length, 3½–7 in
DESCRIPTION Large; prominent eardrums; yellow-green or brown, sometimes blotched
HABITAT Lakes, ponds, slow-flowing streams and rivers
SIMILAR SPECIES Pit Frog also large but its nose more pointed

The Bullfrog is North America's largest frog. Not only is it bigger, it is also more of a predator than most, eating other frogs, small fish, birds, even small snakes in addition to invertebrates; it has a voracious appetite. As a result wherever it has been introduced to places outside of its normal range it has often caused something of a problem, having a negative impact on the pre-existing ecological balance. The Bullfrog spends a lot of time ashore, or very close to it, usually in vegetation; it seems to be less aquatic than most other frogs. Males are territorial during the breeding season and any intruding Bullfrog will face a wrestling match with the resident male. The tadpoles take almost 2 years to metamorphose into frogs, and the young frogs are only mature after 2–3 years.

(HYLA CINEREA) GREEN TREEFROG

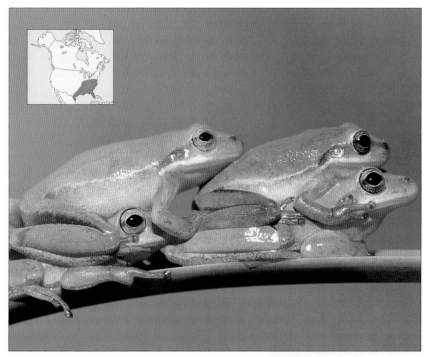

Abundant in densely vegetated swamps and marshes, the Green Treefrog often gathers in large groups by the edges of pools. Nocturnal, it spends the day resting on vegetation without moving, but becomes much more active during the evening, especially if the weather is rainy or damp. It may be attracted to house windows in suburban areas, coming to feed on insects attracted in their turn by the house lights. If the Green Treefrog is disturbed it will make a wild leap into space. Like all treefrogs it is very light, weighing so little that it can be supported by even the thinnest leaves and stems of waterside plants and trees. It has rounded toe pads which act as a climbing aid.

SIZE Length, 1¼–2½ in
DESCRIPTION Slender, long legs, smooth skin; bright green or yellowish green, light stripe along upper jaw and side
HABITAT Well-vegetated; lakes, ponds, streams, swamps
SIMILAR SPECIES Barking Treefrog spotted; Squirrel Treefrog brown, no distinct markings

AMERICAN TOAD
(BUFO AMERICANUS)

Very common, the American Toad is usually found wherever there is moisture and a good source of invertebrates for its food. It is mainly nocturnal and is mostly active from twilight through the evening, especially in warm, rainy weather. It burrows in leaf litter or damp soil during daylight, though it may be more active during the day in spring and fall. It is often found away from water, appearing to only need to be in it for reproduction. During breeding, which happens from spring to summer, males can be heard producing their long, musical, trilling calls. Breeding takes place in ditches, shallow pools, or ponds and – as with other toads – the male holds onto the back of the female and fertilizes the eggs as they are deposited in the water in long strings. Tadpoles develop into toads in 5–10 weeks.

SIZE Length, 2–4 in
DESCRIPTION Large, warty skin; brown gray, or reddish, dark spots, chest often heavily mottled
HABITAT Moist woodland, meadows, marshes, gardens
SIMILAR SPECIES Southern Toad has bony head ridges

ROUGH-SKINNED NEWT
(TARICHA GRANULOSA)

SIZE Length including tail, 5–8½ in
DESCRIPTION Warty; dark brown or gray, bright yellow or orange underside; lower eyelids dark
HABITAT Ponds, lakes, streams; surrounding damp forests and grasslands
SIMILAR SPECIES California Newt has light lower eyelids

Highly aquatic, the Rough-skinned Newt does not go through a terrestrial developmental stage, though it sometimes wanders onto land, moving from the water to adjacent damp habitats particularly after rain or during humid weather. It feeds on a variety of smaller amphibians and their spawn, together with insects and other invertebrates. If it is disturbed it assumes a strange sway-backed defense posture, arching its back and tail to reveal the brightly colored underside. Despite its back not looking as dramatic, the warty skin contains many glands that secrete powerful toxins which can kill most of its predators if swallowed. Some snakes, like garter snakes, are immune and can eat the Rough-skinned Newt with no ill effects.

(NORTHERN) RED SALAMANDER

(PSEUDOTRITON RUBER)

A beautiful and striking amphibian, the Red Salamander closely mimics the highly poisonous, land-dwelling red eft stage of the Eastern Newt as a defense against predation. The Red Salamander has a smooth slimy skin with characteristic grooves along the sides and is larger than the red eft. The adult usually darkens with age, assuming a more purplish color, and the markings gradually become more blotchy and less well defined. It breeds in cold streams running through woodlands, often quite high up, but can be found at lower altitudes in meadows close to water. The young hatch in the fall or even in the winter, and stay in an aquatic larval state for up to 2 years before they become more terrestrial. Males are mature at 4 years, females at 5.

SIZE Length, 4–7 in
DESCRIPTION Bright red with black speckles, yellow eyes and short tail
HABITAT Mountain springs, woodland, lowland streams and meadows
SIMILAR SPECIES Almost identical to Eastern Newt eft stage

TIGER SALAMANDER
(AMBYSTOMA TIGRINUM)

The largest land-dwelling salamander in the world, along with the Pacific Giant Salamander, the Tiger Salamander is seldom seen. It lives in animal burrows or tunnels formed by rotten roots, and spends most of its time underground. It is a voracious predator, eating smaller amphibians, large insects, worms, and other invertebrates. In late winter and spring Tiger Salamanders migrate to their breeding pools and may congregate there in quite large numbers. It is preyed upon by many large fish which has led to anglers using it as bait. This, in its turn, has led to the introduction of the species to many areas outside of its normal range.

SIZE Length, 6–13 in

DESCRIPTION Large; broad rounded head, heavy body; variable color and markings, generally olive and brown marbling with spots and stripes

HABITAT Varies; ponds and surroundings in woodlands, prairie and sagebrush plains

SIMILAR SPECIES Size distinguishes it from others

HELLBENDER (CRYPTOBRANCHUS ALLEGANIENSIS)

SIZE Length, 1–2½ ft

DESCRIPTION Large; flattened head and body, wrinkled skin; gray or brown, often spotted, paler underside

HABITAT Large clear streams and rivers

SIMILAR SPECIES The Mudpuppy has external gills

Strictly aquatic, the Hellbender is one of the largest salamanders; it does not retain its gills through life as some other entirely aquatic salamanders do, however. Though it usually lives in larger bodies of water it generally inhabits the shallows and often hides under large rocks or debris like logs. It propels itself through the water using its flattened tail – the legs are not used for swimming – feeding on crustaceans, mollusks, insects, and worms. It is thought that the Hellbender's wrinkled skin increases its overall surface area, permitting it to absorb more oxygen from the water. Mating takes place in late summer or fall; the eggs, which are laid in long strings, are secured by the female beneath stones or logs. The male guards them until they hatch.

(NECTURUS MACULOSUS) MUDPUPPY

Completely aquatic, the Mudpuppy is also neotenic – retaining larval characteristics, such as its red, feathery, external gills, into adulthood. It may still, however, attain a considerable size and is most often seen by fishermen as it is attracted to worms and fish bait. It feeds on small fish, amphibians, and invertebrates. Active right through the year and generally nocturnal, it may also be active in daylight in some environments, especially deep, muddy ones with lots of dense vegetation. Mating occurs in spring, and the female Mudpuppy may lay more than 100 eggs. These are attached to the underside of submerged rocks or logs, and are guarded by the female until they hatch.

SIZE Length, 8–18 in
DESCRIPTION Large; gray to brown or black, dark red, feathery gills and stripe through each eye
HABITAT Lakes, streams, and rivers
SIMILAR SPECIES None

FISH

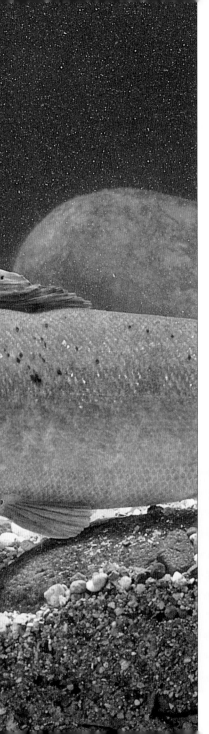

ATLANTIC SALMON
(SALMO SALAR)

The Atlantic Salmon migrates from the sea into freshwater in order to spawn. Starting life in freshwater, some individuals remain in rivers for several years as they develop, before beginning the first stage of the migration to the open sea. After between 1–3 years in the ocean the Atlantic Salmon returns to the river of its birth to spawn in its turn; the journey may be very long indeed. It feeds on small fish and crustaceans while at sea, but stops feeding once it re-enters freshwater. Though it is considerably weaker following spawning it does not generally die, unlike many other species of salmon. It is well-known and well-appreciated as a sport fish, and is renowned for being good to eat; it is also respected for its demanding lifestyle. There are some landlocked Atlantic Salmon populations in several New England states.

SIZE Length up to 4½ ft; weight up to 70 lb (usually less)
DESCRIPTION Dark back, silver sides with small black spots, sometimes in an X shape; during spawning males develop reddish sides and a hooked lower jaw
HABITAT Coastal waters, some rivers and lakes
SIMILAR SPECIES None in range; others are in Pacific

SOCKEYE SALMON (ONCORHYNCHUS NERKA)

SIZE Length up to 30 in; weight up to 15 lb

DESCRIPTION Dramatic coloration in freshwater, bright red with green head; marine coloration blue-green above, silvery below. Females often have green-yellow spots. Snout pointed but blunt

HABITAT Open oceans, streams, rivers, lakes

SIMILAR SPECIES Coloration distinguishes it from other Pacific salmon species

The most distinctive among the several species of salmon found in the Pacific, the Sockeye Salmon is also the most commercially valuable. Like the other Pacific salmon, and the Atlantic Salmon, it migrates from the ocean into river systems for spawning. There are also some landlocked populations where the species has been deliberately introduced. Spawning takes place during summer in small tributary streams or rivers which lead to lakes, and a young salmon spends 1–3 years there before heading out to the sea. A further 2–4 years are spent in the open ocean before it returns to its native stream. Despite its commercial value, few Sockeye Salmon are caught by anglers in the open ocean; it rarely responds to a lure. It is protected in the Pacific northwest, in parts of Washington, Oregon, and Idaho.

(SALVELINUS FONTINALIS) BROOK TROUT

There are numerous species of trout found in North American rivers but the Brook Trout is one of the most popular with anglers. It is widely caught for consumption, unlike the Brown Trout which was introduced to North America in the 19th century. As its name suggests, the Brook Trout most frequently inhabits small, cold streams, often in mountainous regions. Its natural range extends throughout eastern Canada and the Great Lakes southward into the Appalachian Mountains but it is occasionally found close to shore on the Atlantic Coast. It feeds mainly on aquatic insects which it finds along the river bed but it will also eat crayfish and even minnows. The Brook Trout spawns in the fall.

Size Length up to 28 in; weight up to 14 lb

Description Red or yellow hue on back and sides with markings consisting of light stripes and red spots outlined with blue halos.

Habitat Small freshwater streams and tidal streams

Similar Species Arctic Char has red spots

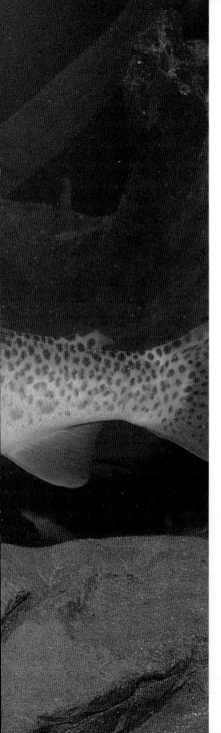

RAINBOW TROUT
(ONCORHYNCHUS MYKISS)

Some Rainbow Trout migrate between their home streams or rivers and the sea when they are 2–4 years old. They remain at sea for a further 3 years or so, until they are sexually mature, then return to their native streams in winter to spawn. These "sea-run" trout are often known as Steelheads and usually lack the reddish side stripe of freshwater individuals; they are silver with blue spots. The freshwater Rainbow Trout is often brilliantly colored all year round and normally spawns in spring. Both types are popular game fish, but the Steelhead populations are often classified as threatened or endangered, largely due to habitat disturbance or pollution. Rainbow Trout are also often raised in aquaculture – they are equally popular with cooks.

SIZE Length up to 3½ ft; weight up to 40 lb

DESCRIPTION Blue-green back, paler underside, silvery flanks with many small dark blotches; in freshwater the spots are more distinct. Stripe along side becomes brighter during spawning

HABITAT Lakes and streams along Pacific but widely introduced elsewhere; some in coastal waters

SIMILAR SPECIES Coloration distinctive; Brook Trout normally smaller

PADDLEFISH (POLYODON SPATHULA)

SIZE Length up to 7 ft; weight up to 200 lb

DESCRIPTION Long, with paddle-shaped snout; mottled blue or gray, belly white; very large mouth; gill covers taper and extend backward

HABITAT Freshwater lakes and backwaters, often murky water

SIMILAR SPECIES None

Probably the most unusual North American fish in terms of appearance, the only other close relative of the Paddlefish is found in China's Yangtze River. Its elongated snout expands into a thick, flat paddle with clear markings. Unscaled, with smooth skin a little like that of a freshwater catfish, it somewhat resembles a basking shark with a long nose, swimming along with its huge mouth open, feeding on plankton as it goes. The Paddlefish can live for up to 30 years. Its range has been much reduced, partly due to overfishing – it is considered to be good eating – and partly due to pollution and other habitat changes such as the building of dams. It is usually caught by fishermen during spawning in late spring or early summer, and its eggs are also eaten as a form of caviar.

(PYLODICTIS OLIVARIS) FLATHEAD CATFISH

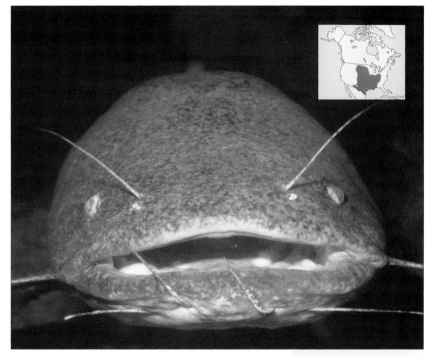

The Flathead Catfish can reach a substantial size, leading to popularity with sport fishermen; it lives in bodies of water where there are places for it to hide among vegetation or general debris. It is also good to eat and has commercial significance in some places, often being deliberately introduced in areas where it is not native. Catfish got their general name because of their "whiskers", barbels around the mouth which are used to detect the presence of food; all North American species have four pairs but those of the Flathead Catfish are rather short proportional to its size. As with all other catfish, the Flathead has a smooth skin; along with its size, the long body, wide, flat head, and broad mouth distinguish it from other species. Young Flathead Catfish eat insects but as they grow their diet changes and they begin to consume other fish and crayfish.

SIZE Length up to 5 ft; weight up to 120 lb

DESCRIPTION Large; back and sides mottled olive green to brown, yellowish belly. Large, flat head, barbels around mouth

HABITAT Freshwater rivers and creeks, often near cover

SIMILAR SPECIES Other freshwater catfish are smaller; Channel Catfish is blue-gray

NORTHERN PIKE
(ESOX LUCIUS)

The Northern Pike, like all pike, is an aggressive and predatory fish. It has a long, powerful body and a large head; its jaws are lined with teeth. Living in freshwater with plentiful aquatic vegetation, it prefers to ambush its prey rather than hunt. It lurks in cover until a suitable target passes, then propels itself toward its victim in a burst of speed. Though pike need vegetation for cover, they have large, high-set eyes and hunt mainly by sight, preferring clean water. In the past there was a commercial pike fishery and it was widely eaten; today it is more valued as a sport fish. There are 5 worldwide species of pike, and 4 are found in North America; out of all of these the Northern Pike is the most widely distributed freshwater fish, being also found in Europe and Asia.

SIZE Length up to 4½ ft; weight up to 46 lb

DESCRIPTION Long, streamlined body, large head, protruding lower jaw; olive green with yellow spots, pale underside, fins pale green, orange, or white

HABITAT Large, slow-moving freshwater rivers and lakes

SIMILAR SPECIES The pickerels are smaller; Muskellunge larger with bars or blotches instead of spots

RAINBOW DARTER (ETHEOSTOMA CAERULEUM)

SIZE Length up to 3 in; weight up to ⅛ oz

DESCRIPTION Olive-black or yellow-green, blue-green belly, 8 darker vertical stripes on sides; fins red with blue edges, that of leading dorsal fin widest

HABITAT Clear freshwater streams and creeks

SIMILAR SPECIES Several similar darters, but all have slight variations in color and pattern. Rainbow Darter fins are distinctive

The striking coloration of the Rainbow Darter has given it the first part of its name; the rapid movements it makes while searching for food have provided the "darter". It eats tiny insects and small crustaceans, hunting along the bottom of fast-flowing streams where the current moves a good supply of food along. It prefers clear, clean water and spawns in clean gravels from May to June. Highly sensitive to pollution levels, the presence or absence of Rainbow Darters can be an indicator of the overall cleanliness of the water. It is a member of the perch family, and though it has a similar body shape to other perch such as the Walleye, it is much smaller and very differently colored.

(CYPRINUS CARPIO) COMMON CARP

The Common Carp was originally introduced from Asia in the late nineteenth century; the US Fish Commission intended that it should become a valuable food fish, but it never became popular. It did, however, become thoroughly at home and is now widespread across North America, though it is more common in warm water. Though it can be a powerful fish, it has never been as widely fished for sport as have some other, native, species. It favors still water, not necessarily clear, over silt or mud with plenty of aquatic plants. It can live in fairly stagnant water; rooting around at the bottom and feeding on invertebrates and vegetation, it will also take insects and weeds from the surface. A closely related species, the Grass Carp, has proved to be detrimental in some places, though it was originally introduced to help control vegetation.

SIZE Length up to 2½ ft; weight up to 60 lb

DESCRIPTION Deep body with very large olive or brass-colored scales; long dorsal fin; two pairs of barbels on upper lip

HABITAT Freshwater streams, ponds, lakes

SIMILAR SPECIES Quillback is similar in appearance but smaller, Smallmouth Buffalo often larger; both lack the barbels

LARGEMOUTH BASS (MICROPTERUS SALMOIDES)

The most popular sport fish in North America, the Largemouth Bass has been widely introduced and flourishes across most of the US. It is the largest freshwater bass. It eats crayfish and smaller fish species, and in some places the introduction of Largemouth Bass has had a severe effect on indigenous fish populations. It lives in a variety of habitats but generally prefers quieter waters which have plenty of aquatic plants. It will live in warmer water, but becomes much less active as the water temperature rises; it also tolerates low levels of salinity. It spawns in the spring and male Largemouth Bass guard the nests – which they make on the bottom – until some days after hatching. The vegetation the fish prefers also helps to provide useful cover for the young.

SIZE Length up to 3 ft; weight up to 22 lb
DESCRIPTION Large, heavy body; olive green in color with dark, diamond-shaped markings on sides; mouth extremely large, extending to below eye
HABITAT Warm, quiet ponds, lakes, river pools with vegetation
SIMILAR SPECIES The Smallmouth Bass grows to about 2 ft; lacks side markings

BURBOT (LOTA LOTA)

SIZE Length up to 3 ft; weight up to 18 lb

DESCRIPTION Long body, flat, broad head; olive to yellowish-brown in color with mottled sides; single barbel on chin

HABITAT Cold, deep, freshwater lakes and rivers

SIMILAR SPECIES Atlantic Tomcod may enter freshwater, but is much smaller

The Burbot is widespread but not common, and is the only member of the cod family, the Gadidae, to live exclusively in freshwater. It is also unusual in that it spawns in winter. As it generally lives in cold northern waters, usually in large bodies of water, this means that it is usually spawning under ice; sometimes, however, it will live in smaller streams. The eggs are unattended and lie on gravel, sand, or rocks at the bottom; they generally hatch after 2 months. The Burbot feeds on fish and crayfish, while the young Burbot eats insects and their larvae. Burbots are infrequently caught by sport fishermen; they hide themselves well among any underwater structures or any other cover that they can find.

(ANGUILLA ROSTRATA) AMERICAN EEL

The American Eel is essentially nocturnal and scavenges for food during the night; in daytime it hides up among debris or in hollows. It spawns in the Sargasso Sea, where the eggs hatch into larvae which pass through successive defined stages before developing into elvers, young eels. This process may take many years, and some parts of it continue to be researched. It is believed that male American Eels remain in coastal waters, while only the females ascend freshwater rivers – and will even move overland to search for water if necessary – where they stay until they reach sexual maturity. At this point most return to the sea for spawning in their turn. Fishermen catch freshwater eels; they are eaten both fresh and smoked.

SIZE Length up to 5 ft
DESCRIPTION Snake-like body, large head, projecting lower jaw; dark back, yellow-brown sides, paler belly
HABITAT Brackish water or freshwater along coast; spawns at sea
SIMILAR SPECIES Lampreys are similar in shape but lack lower jaw

INVERTEBRATES

CABBAGE WHITE
(PIERIS RAPAE)

SIZE Wingspan, 2 in
DESCRIPTION White, black or dark-gray forward wingtips; each forewing has 1 or 2 spots; underside yellowish, mottled with gray
HABITAT Varied, open grassland to urban areas
SIMILAR SPECIES None; other whites usually lack yellow underside or have dark-veined undersides

The Cabbage White is both very common and widespread and is often regarded as a pest; they can be very destructive to crops as they are so plentiful, and will frequently inflict severe damage on garden plants. It is not a native species and was introduced from Europe unintentionally; since then it has flourished across almost all of North America though it is sometimes still referred to as the European Cabbage White. The larvae of the species are often found feeding greedily on cabbages – as the name might suggest – but are also found on other vegetables, especially other brassicas, clover, and similar plants.

COMMON/CLOUDED SULPHUR
(COLIAS PHILODICE)

A familiar and widespread butterfly, the Common or Clouded Sulphur is often seen in groups which gather to drink around puddles. It lives in a variety of grassy habitats, and it is believed that agriculture has enabled the range expansion of this species. The larvae can be fairly destructive to crops of clover, alfalfa, and vegetables whenever they are present in particularly high numbers. The Common or Clouded Sulphur caterpillars usually spend winter in the pupal stage, but eggs can be laid throughout the year and, as a consequence, adults can emerge during much of it.

Size Wingspan, 2 in
Description Pale yellow, both sets of wings bordered with black or brown, less noticeable in females; small dark spot on each forewing, small orange spot on each hindwing
Habitat Open grasslands and clover meadows
Similar species Alfalfa Butterfly (also called Orange Sulphur) orange or deep yellow, otherwise similar

BLACK SWALLOWTAIL
(PAPILIO POLYXENES)

The Black Swallowtail is the most widespread swallowtail butterfly in North America, occurring as far north as parts of Canada. Swallowtails are some of the largest and most beautifully colored of all butterflies; they get their descriptive general name from the "tail" projecting backwards from the hindwings which can be very long in some species. The Black Swallowtail is most notable for its spectacular coloring; its "tail" is short compared to some. The Black Swallowtail caterpillars may become something of a pest to gardeners, as they feed on carrots and other vegetables.

SIZE Wingspan, 4 in
DESCRIPTION Mainly black, but with distinctive blue, red, and yellow markings on wings; yellow spots along body
HABITAT Open habitats, woodland edges, gardens
SIMILAR SPECIES Coloration distinctive

PAINTED LADY
(VANESSA CARDUI)

The Painted Lady is not present in most of North America during winter; it belongs to a group of butterflies known as the brush-footed butterflies which is not particularly tolerant of cold conditions. The brush-footeds derive their name from their short, hairy front legs which they use for tasting, and they are widespread in most appropriate parts of the world. The Painted Lady migrates northwards in summer from warmer, southern places, including Mexico; it may go as far north as Canada. Adults feed on nectar from various flowering plants, but the caterpillars are most frequently found on thistles.

SIZE Wingspan, 2–2½ in

DESCRIPTION Orange with dark forewing edges and wingtips, white spots; hindwing rear edge has small blue and black spots; underside dusky pink with olive, black, and white pattern

HABITAT Varied; meadows, mountains, and gardens to desert

SIMILAR SPECIES American Painted Lady has 2 large eyespots on underside of wings

RED ADMIRAL (VANESSA ATALANTA)

SIZE Wingspan, 1½–2½ in

DESCRIPTION Dark brown or black, white spots on wingtips; orange-red bars across forewings and hindwing edges

HABITAT Parks, gardens, meadows, forest edges, shorelines

SIMILAR SPECIES None

Very easily identifiable, and equally common, the Red Admiral migrates northwards in spring and summer, as does the Painted Lady. It moves from southwestern states where it is a year-round inhabitant to disperse throughout almost all of North America. Juvenile Red Admirals sometimes overwinter in the north in the pupal stage and on occasion, when conditions are very mild, some adults may well also remain in northern parts; otherwise they return to the south. Adults feed on the nectar of various flowers as well as fruit, and the spiny Red Admiral caterpillars are most often found on nettles.

(EVERES COMYNTAS) EASTERN TAILED-BLUE

Despite the name, the Eastern Tailed-blue is actually found right across North America, from the Pacific to the Atlantic, and north to southern Canada. It is more common east of the Rockies, where it is one of the most numerous species. Adult Eastern Tailed-blues may be seen at any time from spring to late summer or fall, and they may well reproduce on successive occasions during this period. The females that emerge early in the season are often more brightly colored than the individuals appearing toward the end of summer. The eggs and larvae develop on the flowers of leguminous vegetables or clover, and the caterpillar may overwinter inside a bean pod.

Size Wingspan, 1 in
Description Small; silvery-blue, dark wing margin with white edge; thin "tails" present on hindwings, with small orange and black spots just above them; female more gray or brown
Habitat Open meadows and gardens
Similar species Western Tailed-blue is slightly larger

POLYPHEMUS MOTH (ANTHERAEA POLYPHEMUS)

SIZE Wingspan, 4–6 in
DESCRIPTION Large; sandy color; large, feathery antennae; eyespots on each wing, hindwing spots are larger, edged in blue
HABITAT Varied; deserts, forests, suburban areas
SIMILAR SPECIES Unmistakable

The Polyphemus Moth is large and distinctive, common throughout the east of North America in a wide range of habitats. The adult moth does not feed, but the caterpillars do, and are found on a variety of trees and plants; they are equally easy to recognize. They are plump and bright green in color, with red and gray tubercles, and may grow to be more than 3 inches long. Along with the caterpillars of some other related species, those of the Polyphemus Moth are known as giant silkworms: when mature they spin large silken cocoons in which to pupate.

(ACTIAS LUNA) LUNA MOTH

The Luna Moth is spectacularly beautiful and distinctive and is very easily recognized by the long "tails" which trail elegantly from its hindwings. It is, however, rarely seen; it is a both a nocturnal forest inhabitant and short-lived. Though the Luna Moth is not presently classified as endangered, it is believed that populations have suffered badly from the use of pesticides. Luna Moth caterpillars are most commonly found on or near walnut or hickory trees, though they usually come down and pupate on the ground among piles of leaf litter.

Size Wingspan, 3–4½ in
Description Large white body, pale green wings with yellow eyespots; forewings have brown or purple leading edge; long "tails" are present on hindwings
Habitat Broadleaf woodlands
Similar species None

COMMON GREEN DARTER/ DARNER
(ANAX JUNIUS)

One of the largest and most frequently seen dragonflies in North America, the Common Green Darter – or Green Darner as it is also known – is widespread from coast to coast, though more common in the east. A powerful flyer, an adult Common Green Darter is often seen as it hunts, chasing flying insects or mosquitoes at the edges of lakes or ponds. The male is strongly territorial and chases away other males during the breeding season. After mating the female deposits her eggs one by one onto the stems of aquatic plants, and the nymphs live an aquatic life for about a year; they feed on tadpoles, small fish and insects and emerge from the water to transform as the weather gets warmer in spring or summer.

SIZE Length, 3 in; wingspan, 4½ in
DESCRIPTION Large; bright green head and thorax, blue or purplish abdomen, clear wings
HABITAT Marshes, vegetated ponds, lakes, slow-moving streams
SIMILAR SPECIES Heroic Darner is larger

CIVIL BLUET

(ENALLAGMA CIVILE)

SIZE Length, 1–1¼ in; wingspan, 1¼–1½ in

DESCRIPTION Bright blue in color; black markings on abdomen; transparent wings

HABITAT Near still or slow-moving water, often with abundant vegetation

SIMILAR SPECIES Northern Bluet is more robust

On of the most common and widespread damselflies in North America, the Civil Bluet is also known as the Familiar Bluet. It is one of a group of small, mainly blue damselflies. The female is frequently much duller in color, often being gray to brown. The Civil Bluet is most frequently spotted along sandy shorelines close to vegetation as it hunts for the small flying insects that make up its diet. Adults usually fly from May to October and breeding pairs are sometimes seen, flying together, through the summer months. The eggs are deposited inside the soft stems of some aquatic plants, and hatch into predatory aquatic larvae.

AMERICAN/
(LUCANUS ELEPHAS) ELEPHANT STAG BEETLE

Feeding as it does on the sap of trees and leaves, the American Stag Beetle is completely harmless although it looks large and quite alarming. In woodland areas it is often found close to decaying trees; in suburbs it may be attracted to windows and any other sources of light. The "antlers" are used during breeding, to tip rival males over on to their backs. The large white larval grub develops in a damp forest environment, generally living in a rotting stump or log for a year or more before it emerges as a winged adult in the summer.

SIZE Length, 1½–2 in

DESCRIPTION Large; reddish-brown to black; enlarged mandibles; male's are antler-like, may be 1 in long

HABITAT Woodland, grassland, suburban areas

SIMILAR SPECIES Eastern Hercules Beetle usually yellowish, three projections on head

TWO-SPOTTED LADY (BIRD/BUG) BEETLE (ADALIA BIPUNCTATA)

SIZE Length, ⅛–¼ in

DESCRIPTION Small; red, black and white head and thorax, black spot on each wing

HABITAT Woodland, meadows, gardens

SIMILAR SPECIES Distinguished from others by number of spots

An easily identified and very familiar beetle, called either a Lady, a Ladybird, or a Ladybug Beetle. It is popular with gardeners because it consumes large numbers of aphids and other plant-damaging insect pests. It can sometimes be found hibernating in buildings in the northern part of its range, in houses or in other places providing shelter, and often in large numbers. Outside of these areas, breeding takes place throughout the year. The eggs are laid on the underside of leaves or on plant stems, and the Two-spotted also pupates in such places. The larvae, which are elongated in shape and mainly black with white and yellow spots, also eat aphids.

CARPENTER ANT
(CAMPONOTUS PENNSYLVANICUS)

The Carpenter Ant is heavily built, which makes it relatively easy to identify. Ants are close relatives of wasps and live in communal, highly organized nests comprising many hundreds of individuals. This ant does not eat the wood in which it is found; it tunnels through it to form its communal nest and may cause considerable and extensive damage to property. It eats fruits, nectar, and insects but gets most of its energy by "milking" aphids of their honeydew. As with all ants, most Carpenters are wingless workers – collecting food, protecting the nest and larvae – and will deliver a painful bite if disturbed. Reproductive individuals are produced periodically; they leave the nest to breed and establish new colonies. They are winged and mate during swarming flights.

Size Length, up to ½ in
Description Large, entirely black
Habitat In wood, sometimes wood in buildings
Similar species Size distinguishes it from others

EASTERN SUBTERRANEAN
TERMITE (RETICULITERMES FLAVIPES)

SIZE Length, ¼ in
DESCRIPTION Ant-like, but without thin waist; workers cream or white, soldiers slightly larger with dark head and strong jaws, reproductives winged and black
HABITAT Soil and wood in damp forests, buildings
SIMILAR SPECIES None in range

Eastern Subterranean Termite colonies can be huge, sometimes with over a million members, and have a highly structured social organization similar to that of wasps, bees, and ants. There are workers, soldiers, and reproductive individuals; the latter may be kings, queens, or alates. Alates are winged and capable of starting a new colony; kings and queens are flightless. Most termites are workers, searching for food, repairing the nest, or tending the larvae. Soldiers guard the nest against intruders like ants, and protect the foraging workers. In their natural habitat, termites – which eat wood – are regarded as beneficial, helping to speed up the process of wood decomposition. In buildings, however, they are one of the most destructive insects in North America.

DIFFERENTIAL GRASSHOPPER
(MELANOPLUS DIFFERENTIALIS)

Possibly the most widespread and common of North American grasshoppers, the Differential Grasshopper is an agricultural pest; when it occurs in sufficient numbers it can devastate crops. It also eats fruit and grasses, and leaps from one plant to another with its long, powerful legs. It is capable of flight, like other grasshoppers, but unlike many it does not migrate. In summer it is at its most numerous, and the distinctive loud buzzing or chirping "singing" can be heard across open grasslands. This sound is produced by it rubbing its legs against its wings. The female lays about 80 eggs in the soil, depositing them in small groups.

Size Length, 1½–1¾ in

Description Short antennae, spines on hind legs; yellow-brown, black markings

Habitat Woodland, meadows, grassland

Similar species Meadow Grasshopper has longer antennae, often found in marshy habitats

PRAYING MANTIS
(MANTIS RELIGIOSA)

A non-native species, the Praying Mantis was accidentally introduced from Europe in the nineteenth century, and is sometimes called the European Praying Mantis as a result. The two front legs are held together as though in prayer, explaining the common name further. These legs are specially adapted for grasping prey and holding on to it once caught. The Praying Mantis eats a variety of smaller insects like moths, butterflies, and their caterpillars, and – as it helps control herbivorous pests – is useful to gardeners. It is also cannibalistic; the female typically eats the male immediately after mating. The eggs, laid in fall, overwinter on the leaves of shrubs and the nymphs emerge in the spring. Though it looks fearsome, it is completely harmless to people.

SIZE Length 2–2½ in
DESCRIPTION Wings reach beyond abdomen; forelegs large with white, black-ringed spot, head triangular; body green or light brown
HABITAT Meadows and gardens
SIMILAR SPECIES Carolina Mantis lacks spots below forelegs

HOUSE FLY
(MUSCA DOMESTICA)

SIZE Length up to ½ in
DESCRIPTION Gray and black striped thorax; dark, hairy abdomen
HABITAT Human habitations, farmland
SIMILAR SPECIES Blow Fly has metallic green abdomen

Common and widespread, the House Fly is notorious for its ability to transmit parasitic worms and disease-causing bacteria; it is known to assist in the spread of such plagues as cholera, typhoid, and tuberculosis. It feeds on sugary foods, as well as other organic matter, often decaying, and is frequently found around garbage and sewage. It liquefies its food by regurgitating saliva onto it; its mouthparts are only designed for sucking up liquids. It can have a very truncated life cycle; the eggs hatch within a day, and both the larval and pupal stages may be complete in a week. Following this, the adults may survive for less than a month; several generations can therefore be produced in one season.

EASTERN YELLOW JACKET
(VESPULA MACULIFRONS)

Notorious for its painful sting, the Yellow Jacket is the most widespread and well-known of the wasp species in North America. It is normally only aggressive if threatened or defending the nest. The Eastern Yellow Jacket usually nests in the ground or in decaying wood, where it builds a delicate-seeming structure from chewed material, but it also nests under house eaves or in wall cavities. It drinks nectar from flowers but also eats carrion, fruit, sugary human food, and smaller insects. Following mating the queens usually overwinter in leaf litter and establish new colonies with sterile female workers in the spring; fertile males and new queens tend not to appear until later. The larvae are fed with pre-chewed food by the workers.

SIZE Length, ½–¾ in
DESCRIPTION Stout body, thorax mainly black, dark wings; yellow and black banded abdomen
HABITAT Woodland, meadows, parks, gardens
SIMILAR SPECIES The Common Yellow Jacket is found across Canada and northeastern US

HONEY BEE
(APIS MELLIFERA)

SIZE Length, ½ in

DESCRIPTION Dark thorax with light hairs; slender orange abdomen with dark bands

HABITAT Woodland, meadows, cultivated fields, gardens

SIMILAR SPECIES American Bumblebee is larger and hairier

A species introduced from Europe, the Honey Bee is widespread and one of the most important insects in North America. Not only does it provide honey, it is also a valuable pollinator of many plants, including a range of fruits and vegetables. It may sting if provoked. Large colonies form within hives, but they revert to the wild easily and may also be found nesting in hollow trees. Workers make up most of the bees in a colony; they are sterile females and maintain the nest, collect pollen, and look after the eggs produced by the colony's queen. During spring or summer the queen may start a new colony and leave the original one, accompanied by a stream of workers. A new queen is left behind with fertile males, known as drones.

BLACK-AND-YELLOW ARGIOPE
(ARGIOPE AURANTIA)

Also known as the Black-and-yellow Garden Spider or Golden Orb Weaver, the Black-and-yellow Argiope is one of the most striking spiders found in North America. Relatively common, widespread, brightly colored, and often quite large, it is consequently easy to see and identify. The female's web is also large and usually spans a gap between plant stems; she is usually visible during the day waiting in the center of her web for any flying insects to become entangled. The male's web is usually smaller and located beside that of the female. The female produces one or more egg cases after mating, each one of which may contain over 1000 eggs. She watches over these until the beginning of winter, when she dies; though the eggs hatch in fall, the young spiders stay inside the cocoon until spring.

SIZE Length, female ¾ in male ¼ in

DESCRIPTION Bold black and yellow coloration on body; legs black and orange

HABITAT Gardens, vegetated areas

SIMILAR SPECIES Silver Argiope has whiter body with black stripes; less widespread

DESERT TARANTULA/ ARIZONA HAIRY MYGALOMORPH

(APHONOPELMA CHALCODES)

An impressive predator also known as the Bird-eating Spider, the Desert Tarantula mostly feeds on large insects, but is perfectly able to overpower and eat small vertebrates such as birds, lizards, and rodents. Though it is nocturnal it does not go far from its burrow even at night until the breeding season, when the male will wander off to look for a mate, tapping tentatively at the silken threads beside the entrances to female burrows. The male retreats immediately after mating to avoid the female's predatory attention. The eggs are laid in the female's burrow and she may stay with them until the young tarantulas hatch and then disperse. Not generally aggressive toward humans, the Desert Tarantula may shed irritating hairs or sting when threatened; the venom is relatively mild and has roughly the same effect on a person as a bee sting.

Size Length, 2–3 in
Description Large; heavy body, very hairy; usually gray-brown to black
Habitat Desert areas
Similar species Trapdoor spiders are smaller and less hairy

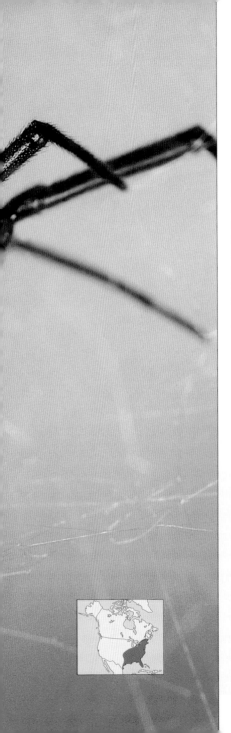

SOUTHERN BLACK WIDOW SPIDER
(LATRODECTUS MACTANS)

Venomous and potentially fatal to humans, the Black Widow Spider is notorious. The female makes a frayed-looking web with a silken tunnel where she spends most of her time; as with most spiders, the males wander about, searching for mates, while the females wait for one to come along. Following mating the female typically eats the male, though a male may occasionally survive to mate with another female. The Southern Black Widow Spider is sometimes found in houses, taking shelter among clothing or inside footwear, but will not generally respond aggressively to disturbance unless it is guarding egg cases. It prefers to fall to the ground and play dead or hide again if at all possible.

SIZE Length, ⅛–¼ in
DESCRIPTION Round abdomen with red marking below in female, male elongated with red and white stripes, both black and shiny; female larger
HABITAT Woodpiles, crevices, vegetation, basements
SIMILAR SPECIES The Western Black Widow is most common from southwestern deserts along Pacific to southern Canada

GIANT (DESERT) HAIRY SCORPION

(HADRURUS ARIZONENSIS)

The largest scorpion found in North America, the Giant (Desert) Hairy Scorpion is venomous. Its large size makes this scorpion look particularly menacing, with its large pincers and long tail terminating in a vicious-looking venomous barb. It has been known to become aggressive and attack humans, but its sting is only rarely fatal. Mainly active at night, it uses the impressively large stinger to both deter any potential predators and subdue its prey; it usually hunts for large insects but will also kill small snakes and lizards, dismembering these in order to consume them.

SIZE Length, 5½–6 in
DESCRIPTION Large; long tail, dark hairs on pincers, legs, and abdomen; yellow-brown with dark back and paler legs
HABITAT Desert valleys
SIMILAR SPECIES None; size makes it distinctive

INDEX OF COMMON NAMES

INDEX OF SCIENTIFIC NAMES

Picture Credits

The publisher would like to thank Photolibrary.com for providing the photographs for this book. We would also like to thank the following for their kind permission to reproduce their photographs:

AA 187; A&S Carey 38; Alain Christof 114; Alan G Nelson 139; Alan Root/SAL 15; Andreas Hartl/Okapia 207; Ben Osborne 109; Bill Paton 132; Bob Bennett 97; Bob Rozinski 124; Breck P Kent 32,141, 176, 245; Brian Kenney 195, 225, 227; C C Lockwood/AA 77; Chris Sharp 152; Claude Steelman/SAL 56,175; D J Saunders 230 (and front cover, center); D&M Zimmerman 74; Daniel Cox, 12/13, 47,49, 60, 62, 64, 94/95, 96, 208, 243; David M Dennis 164, 172, 198, 202, 232; Daybreak Imagery 231; Dennis Green 128; Donald Specker 239, 244; Dr F Ehrenstrom & L Beyer 215, 220; E R Degginger/AA 241; Eric Woods 107; Frank Huber 100; Frank Schneidermeyer 89 157; Fred Whitehead 42; Hans Reinhard 159; Harold Taylor 238; Harry Engels/AA 79; Henry R Fox/AA 105, Herb Segars/AA 93, Howard Hall 66 87, 169; Gregory Brown/AA 209; J&F Burek/AA 221; James H Robinson 240; James Robinson 131; Joe Mcdonald/AA 40 194; Joe McDonald/OKAPIA 86; John Downer 103; John Gerlach/AA 26; John Gerlack Fisher 158; John Mitchell 233; Judd Cooney 72; Ken Cole 143; Kenneth Day 149; Konrad Wothe 108, 113; Leonard Lee Rue III/AA, 91; Leonard Lee Rue III/AA, 162; Lon E Lauber 110, 117; Maresa Pryor/AA, 25; Mark Hamblin 23 (and back flap), 27, 115, 127; Marty Cordano 201 (and back cover), 249; Mary Plage 42, 119; Matthius Breiter 118, 59 Michael Cox 68 70; Mike & Elvan Habicht/AA 16; Mike Hill 133; Mike Price 140; Niall Benvie 24; Norbert Wu 212; Oliver Grunewald 167; OSF 177, 180, 192; Paul Franklin 229; Prof Jack Dermid 181, 203, 247; Ray Richardson/AA 75; Raymond Mendez/AA, 160/161, 216; Richard Day 134, 135, 137, 138, 149; Richard Kolar/AA 193; Richard Packwood 106, 125, 142; Ronald Toms 35, 44; Rudie Kuiter 211, 217; Scott Camazine 235, 251; Stan Osilinski 19,34,37, 98, 102, 122, 123, 129, 163, 165, 189; Steve Turner 51; Susan Beatty/AA 42; Tom Edwards 151; Tom Ulrich 14, 20, 38, 64, 66, 81, 84, 116, 147, 148, 155; Tony Martin 57; Tony Tilford 153, Victoria Mccormick/AA 53, 204/5; W Shantil & B Rozinski 55 (and front cover, left); William Gray 99; Zig Leszczynski 21, 83, 171, 183, 185, 191, 197, 199, 219

Catfish on page 213 © Pat Morris/Ardea